OFF THE WALL
at
SARDI'S

VINCENT SARDI, JR.
&
THOMAS EDWARD WEST

APPLAUSE
B O O K S
211 W. 71st St, New York, NY 10023

This book is lovingly dedicated to Eugenia Pallera Sardi and Vincent Sardi, Sr.

HAMLET: Good my lord, will you see the players well bestowed? Do you hear, let them be well used; for they are the abstract and brief chronicles of the time. After your death, you were better have a bad epitaph than their ill report while you live.

POLONIUS: My lord, I will use them according to their desert.

HAMLET: God's bodykins, man, much better! Use every man after his desert, and who shall scape whipping: use them after your own honor and dignity. The less they deserve, the more merit is in your bounty. Take them in.

Hamlet, II,ii

• • •

LUCILIUS: They mean this night in Sardis to be quartered.

Julius Caesar, IV, ii

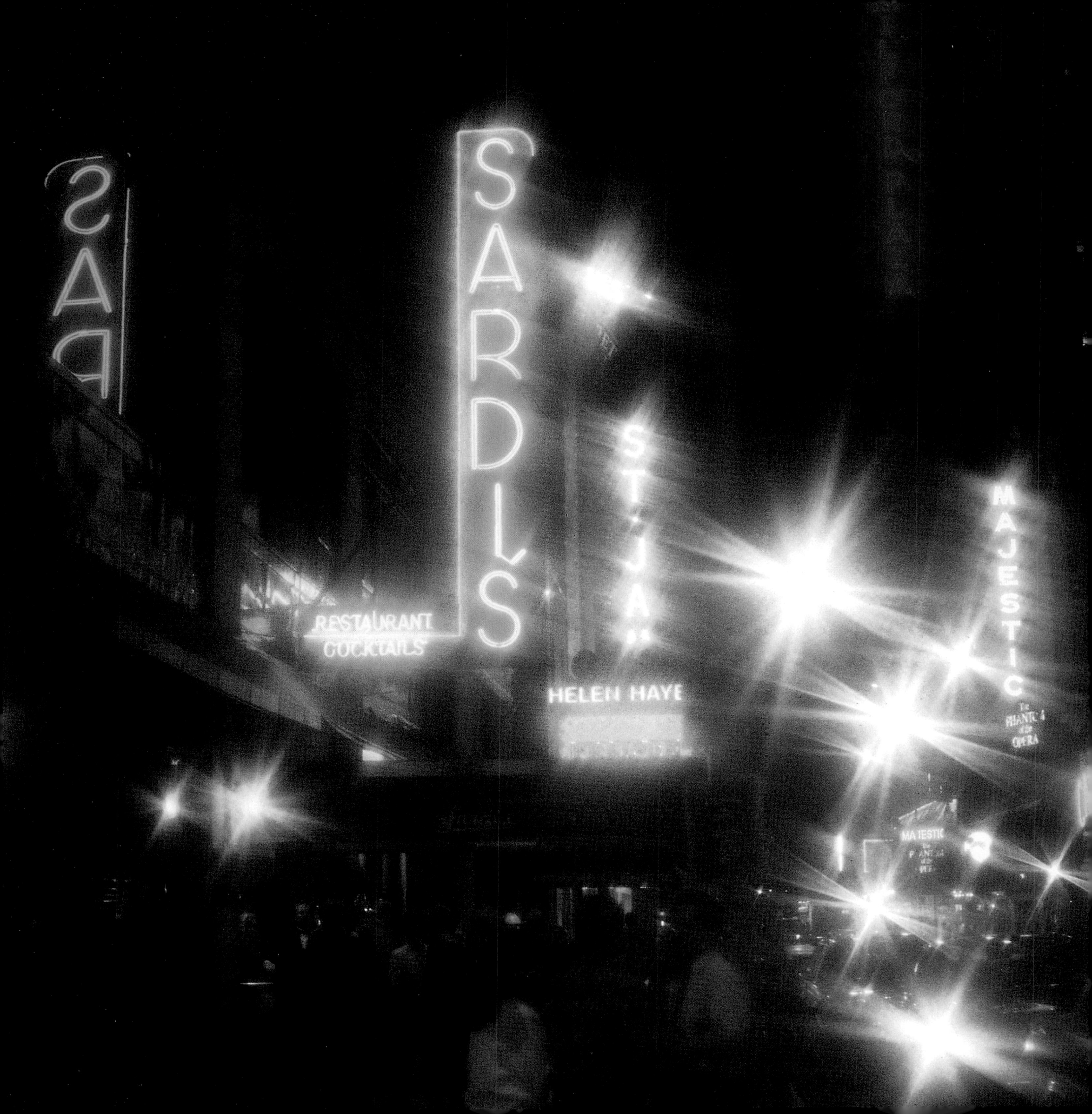
SARDI'S
RESTAURANT
COCKTAILS
HELEN HAYE
MAJESTIC

ACKNOWLEDGEMENTS:

Special thanks to V. Max Klimavicius and The Shubert Organization for the revival of Sardi's Restaurant.

Vincent Sardi, Jr.

The original idea and title for *Off The Wall At Sardi's* came from Marion Rowen. Principal photography by Antonio Rosario. Additional photography by Thomas Palumbo. Graphic design by Toby Welles of Design Core. Special thanks to: Bob Taylor, Curator of the Billy Rose Collection, New York Public Library at Lincoln Center, and Brian O'Connell, Steve Vallillo, Kevin Chamberlain and the rest of the staff at the Lincoln Center Library; Lloyd Kamphorst, Production Coordinator; George Peldys; Velma Tio; Jane MacPherson; John Tay; Carol Mack; V. Max Klimavicius, Mitchell Albert, George Spicijaric, Richard Sherman, and the rest of the "family" at Sardi's; Don Bevan, Richard Baratz, Tamara Geva, Tabitha Sardi and Anne Sardi Gina, for sharing memories and memorabilia; Jay Poynor for creative agentry; Mr. and Mrs. Edward E. West for all manner of support; Glenn Young for faith, fortitude and dedication; and, most of all, to Alana, for encouragement, assistance, patience and devotion above and beyond the call.

Thomas Edward West

Library of Congress Cataloging-in-Publication Data
Sardi, Vincent, 1915-
Off the Wall at Sardi's : Broadway's unofficial hall of fame /
by Vincent Sardi Jr., Thomas Edward West.
p. cm.
"With over 250 caricatures by Alex Gard, John Mackey, Don Bevan, and Richard Baratz."
"An Applause original" — T.p. verso.
ISBN 1-55783-051-7 : $35.00
1. Theater — New York (N.Y.) — Caricatures and cartoons.
2. Motion picture actors and actresses — United States — Caricatures and cartoons.
3. Sardi's (Restaurant) — History. I. West, Thomas Edward.
II. Gard, Alex. III. Sardi's (Restaurant) IV. Title.
741.5'97471 — dc20
91-34476   CIP

APPLAUSE BOOKS
211 W. 71st St.
New York, NY 10023
212-595-4735, Fax: 212-721-2856

Printed by Burch, Benton Harbor, Michigan.
Color film supplied by Scantrans.
Typesetting by Graffolio, La Crosse, Wisconsin.

For over seventy years now, since I was five, Sardi's has served as the club, mess hall, lounge, post office, saloon and marketplace of the American theater. We're right in the heart of the theater district, next to *The New York Times* and across from Shubert Alley. A lot of restaurants on the Rialto have come and gone, but Sardi's still remains a message center, a lovers' rendezvous, a production office, a casting center, and even a psychiatrist's couch. We serve food, too.

Sardi's is one of the few restaurants in New York to have survived relatively unchanged since the 1920's. Of course, we've spruced up, redecorated, kept things up to date, but you can still step in here and be whisked back to another time. Like Rick's Café Americain in *Casablanca*, everybody comes to Sardi's sooner or later, and if you've made your mark, you'll be up on the wall. I've seen the most hard-bitten, cynical New Yorkers come into Sardi's and act like rubbernecking tourists, and for good reason. Hanging on the walls of Sardi's is Broadway's unofficial Hall of Fame. The biggest names in the business are all here … well, almost. You won't find Alfred Lunt and Lynn Fontanne, for example. Alfred was a better cook than the chefs in most restaurants, and the Lunts hardly ever dined out. In order for us to do your caricature, stardom is good, but it helps

to be a regular customer. Over the decades, a lot of famous people got more than dinner at Sardi's: they got credit; found jobs; fell in love; celebrated marriages, affairs and divorces; got standing ovations and saw careers come apart; and the most fortunate got their caricatures hung on the walls and became part of the Sardi's "family." Carol Channing once said, "My family has had birthday and wedding parties at Sardi's for years. I plan on having my funeral there."

We keep two menus at Sardi's: the "Actors' Menu" is for bona fide theater professionals; the regular menu (and regular prices) is for everyone else. Of course, we get a lot of visitors to New York who want to tell the folks back home that they saw *Miss Saigon* and *Phantom of the Opera* and then went to Sardi's. These "outsiders" come to Sardi's to sit cheek by jowl with the "insiders," the official members of the club: the actors, actresses, playwrights, producers, directors, designers, press agents and other denizens of the drama who call Sardi's their second home.

When Mother and Dad opened the restaurant in its current location in 1927, the building was owned by Lee and J.J. Shubert. In fact, it's still owned by the Shubert Organization. Well, Dad went through a period where he wasn't getting along with

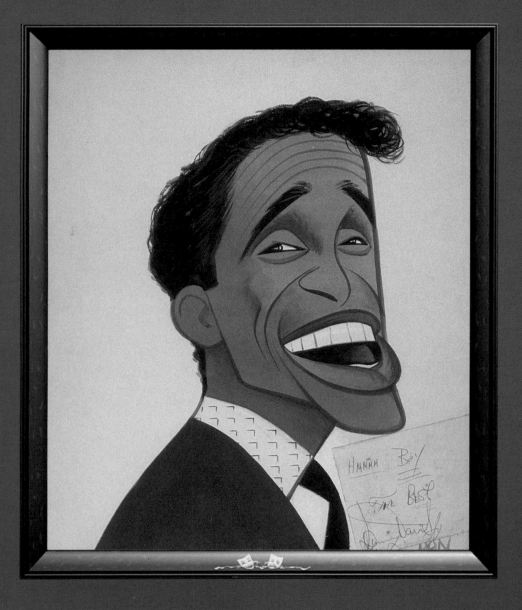

DON
BEVAN

For dear Vincent and
his Institution!
with love and
gratitude,
Carol Channing

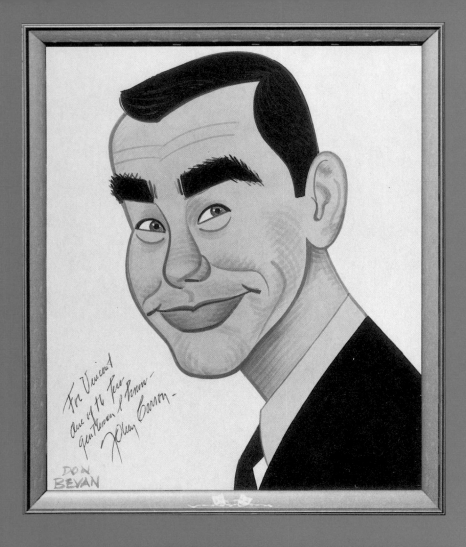

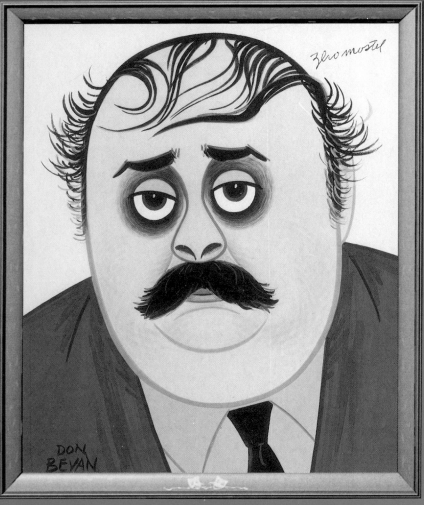

the brothers. He was struggling, and I'm sure the Shuberts' accountants were pretty tough on him. The lease said that the landlords owned all the fixtures, which included anything "permanently attached to the walls." So Dad had the caricatures loosely mounted so that they weren't "permanently attached." Just in case Dad lost his lease, he wanted to take them with him. Needless to say, we're still here, and so are the caricatures.

A lot of famous people are loath to come back after being out of town, for fear of where their caricature may have ended up. The caricatures aren't in fixed positions. We do move them around. When an actor comes back to town, we make every effort to move him up front. Likewise, if you're opening in a show, we move you up near the front door and try to keep you there for the run of the play. Normally, we wait until after the opening to do caricatures of cast members we don't have.

Your position on the wall has nothing to do with your real status, but you know actors' egos. Back when *Bells Are Ringing* was playing — you remember, the musical about the answering service — Jule Styne did the score, Comden and Green the book and lyrics, Judy Holliday was the star? Well, I wanted to have our artist Don Bevan caricature Judy Holliday, but Miss Holliday was a very gracious lady and wanted her co-star, Sydney Chaplin, Charlie's son, to be done, too. Well, Chaplin found out that once his caricature was on the walls, it would be moved around. He asked me, "You mean, if I'm in a flop, you'll move me to the men's room?" Chaplin refused to be done, and he actually convinced Judy Holliday to refuse, too. She cried about it, but she was never done.

Some of the caricatures have been stolen over the years, too. Kirk Douglas's has vanished; so has the original one of producer David Merrick. I'm told that Anna Maria Alberghetti, who starred in *Carnival* for Merrick, hated the producer so much that she stole his caricature and hung it in her bathroom, right above the toilet. As far as I know, it's still there.

Maureen Stapleton stole her caricature — even though friends like Marlon Brando, Eli Wallach and Anne Jackson thought it was terrific. I thought so, too, but she just couldn't stand it. So one day, while no one was looking, she lifted it, took it home and burned it. Then, being embarrassed, for the longest time she wouldn't come back to Sardi's. Finally, I sent her a telegram. It said, "All is forgiven — come home. Father

PREVIOUS PAGES: SAMMY DAVIS JR., LUCILLE BALL, GEORGE BURNS, CAROL CHANNING

THIS PAGE: JOHNNY CARSON, ZERO MOSTEL

Sardi." She came back. But the caricature is gone forever, and she won't let me do another.

As a rule, no caricature goes on the wall unless the subject signs it; the artist isn't paid until it's signed, either. So, you see, it's not as if I just decided to put, say, Bette Davis up there, whether she liked it or not. She had to come in here enough to earn the honor, and then she had to sign the caricature whether she liked it or not.

Not that all the faces are big stars. There are a lot of character people, too. You may not know their names, but you'll know their faces. And there are producers, directors, choreographers, writers, even designers. Abe Feder, the lighting designer, signed his, "Is there enough light on me?"

I've made some mistakes over the years. Some young actor will make a show-stopping splash in a single role. I'll get caught up in the star-is-born syndrome, and before you know it, he'll fade away. The only artifact of that burgeoning career will be the caricature. But, in general, you have to make your mark pretty indelibly on stage or screen before you make it to the walls of Sardi's.

We did Betty Perske a few years after she stopped selling papers in front of Sardi's — but only after she became Lauren Bacall. Kirk Douglas signed his, "And to think they wouldn't let me into this joint once." Jessica Tandy, when she was done — after she'd become a tremendous sensation as Blanche DuBois, no less — signed hers, "Now I know that I have arrived."

T he story of Sardi's really begins at the Bartholdi Inn, a boarding house for what used to be called "theatricals," which stood at Broadway and 45th Street. Carved out of seven brownstone houses, it was the classiest such establishment of its time. Madama Theresa Bartholdi offered her best rooms at the princely sum of twelve dollars a week to matinee idols like Maurice Costello and John Drew. The Bartholdi Inn is where my parents met in 1907. They'd both come to this country from the same region of northern Italy — Mother directly, Dad by way of London.

Before the movies moved to Hollywood, the center of the film industry was exotic Fort Lee, New Jersey. Until Sarah Bernhardt made a movie, most "legit" actors would rather work in a flea circus than appear before a camera. One actor who lived in the Bartholdi — a Southerner and a bit of a snob to boot — was by all accounts a truly terrible actor. He couldn't get a job on

THIS PAGE: EDDIE CANTOR, JEROME KERN

FOLLOWING PAGE: LAUREN BACALL, YUL BRYNNER,
                        SIDNEY POITIER, CAROL BURNETT

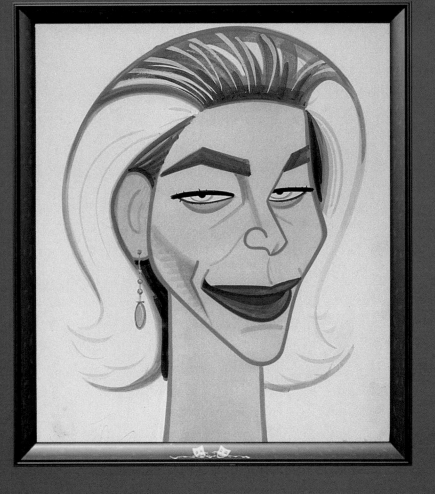

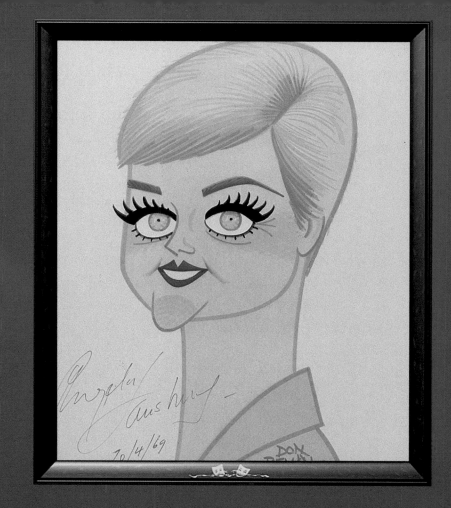

Angela Lansbury
30/4/69

To Sardi's
Sincerely
Lena Horne

DON
BEVAN

I don't know what
to write anymore
there days, but
who'll read what I write
anyway?
Harry Belafonte

DON
BEVAN

stage, so he tried acting in the movies, but he was terrible at that, too. He tried writing plays, but without any success.

With options rapidly dwindling, he thought he'd try his hand at directing pictures. And he did, too. Here's his caricature: D.W. Griffith. He was always kind to my parents on his way up, and they were kind to him on his way down. By the time he returned to New York, Griffith was a pariah in Hollywood, and was hitting the bottle. But Dad always called him "Mr. Griffith" and treated him with the respect he couldn't get anywhere else. Notice how he signed his caricature "O.K., D.W." as if he were approving a production design for one of his movies.

Griffith wasn't the only movie pioneer living at the Bartholdi Inn. Mack Sennett, Mary Pickford, William S. Hart (a Shakespearean actor whose biggest triumph was as Messala in the stage version of Ben-Hur before he became a movie cowboy), and the "Queen of the Serials" herself, Pearl White, all took up residence there. Another Bartholdi actor, a big, beefy fellow, was making a series of slapstick comedies, in "drag" as a Swedish maid, no less: Wallace Beery.

Behind the scenes of the Bartholdi Inn, a love story worthy of one of Griffith's Biograph one-reelers was unfolding. Brown-eyed, dark-haired, strikingly beautiful Eugenia Pallera was the chief housekeeper at the Bartholdi Inn. Across a crowded (dining) room gazed the Italian waiter who loved Jenny, the mustachioed Melchiorre Pio Vincenzo Sardi, nicknamed "Cencin" (pronounced "chen-chin"). Cencin adored his "Cita" — which meant "dear little one" — so much that even Jenny's casual mention that she liked fresh peaches sent him racing to the nearest fruit market to buy her a bushel.

He proposed; she refused. She wouldn't marry him because she didn't like his mustache. They fought; he lost. Cencin went to Pittsburgh to forget. But he neither forgot his Cita nor found work. In Pittsburgh in those days, a waiter with a mustache could only get a job in Italian or French restaurants, and he'd tried every one of them in the Iron City. In despair, he shaved off his mustache and sent it to Jenny as an emblem of his desperate devotion to her.

The mustache apparently tickled her fancy; when Vincent (as he now called himself) returned to New York, Eugenia was very happy to see him. But there was "another man," or men, in this case: the executives of the Pathé film company, producers of The Perils of Pauline. These producers wanted to launch the photogenic Jenny as "the next Pearl White." She had never acted in her life.

Vincent had forsaken Pittsburgh for Jenny. She preferred Pathé. "Let's go for a walk," he said, and Nature's special

effects team cut in, in the form of a teeming rainstorm. They ran for cover in a doorway at Seventh Avenue and 53rd Street. She huddled close; he put his arm around her and once again he proposed.

At Holy Cross Church on West 42nd Street — Father Duffy's church — on June 19, 1911, the waiter and the starlet-that-never-would-be were married. Jenny flubbed her first rehearsed line when she promised to love Vincent "in sickness and in hell." Before long, a daughter, Anne, came along, followed by yours truly on July 23, 1915.

To feed four mouths, Dad worked three jobs: lunch at Lord & Taylor's, dinner at the Yale Club, and the after-hours shift at the Shuberts' Montmartre nightclub on the roof of the Winter Garden. The Shuberts controlled about seventy-five percent of the legitimate theaters in the country at the time. The Montmartre was a popular haunt for the likes of Al Jolson, Diamond Jim Brady and a swarthy tango dancer/gigolo that nobody trusted named Rudolph Valentino. The Montmartre featured lavish revues; the tips were as extravagant as the chorus girls' costumes were infinitesimal.

There were originally three Shuberts — Sam, Lee and Jacob (J.J.). They'd come from Syracuse to conquer the New York theater. Most people don't realize that the title of the Rodgers and Hart/George Abbott musical The Boys From Syracuse was an affectionate poke at the Shuberts. After Sam S. Shubert was killed in a train wreck in 1905, Lee and J.J. carried on the dynasty. Lee, whose face was always likened to that of the Indian on the old nickel, is the only Shubert on the walls at Sardi's. J.J. never consented, possibly after he'd seen what fate had met his brother, Lee.

PREVIOUS PAGE: ANGELA LANSBURY, LENA HORNE,
                 HARRY BELAFONTE

THIS PAGE: EUGENIA PALLERA SARDI

FACING PAGE: ETHEL BARRYMORE, D.W. GRIFFITH,
                 LEE SHUBERT

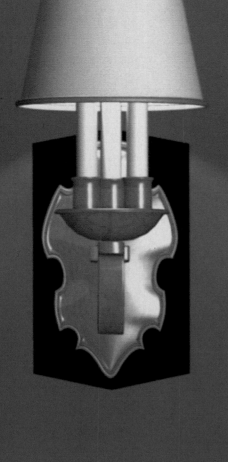

By 1921, Rudolph Valentino was the rage of the country as "The Sheik"; Dad and Mother had ambitions of their own. Right on cue, a friend who owned a small restaurant moved to larger quarters, and offered them the lease on the space at 146 West 44th Street, where our story officially begins. They called it "The Little Restaurant." And it *was* little, but its name actually refers to Winthrop Ames's "Little Theater" next door, which today is the "new" Helen Hayes Theater. The "old" Helen Hayes Theater (which was called the Fulton Theater before it was re-named for Helen Hayes) used to be where the Marriott Marquis Hotel is now. Got all that?

We lived over the restaurant. The backyard, which was fitted up as a garden dining room, was also home to my dog, my cat, and my rabbits. When Mother and Dad weren't looking, I'd sell customers lettuce so they could feed the rabbits. I always had some little business going. I went to grammar school at Holy Cross on 42nd Street, but I ate my lunch at the restaurant, and then smuggled back French pastries for the nuns. And they'd pay me for them! I even remember sneaking in an entire lobster stew. I lived in constant dread that my catering career would be cut short by a priest!

Winthrop Ames, the well-known producer, always brought

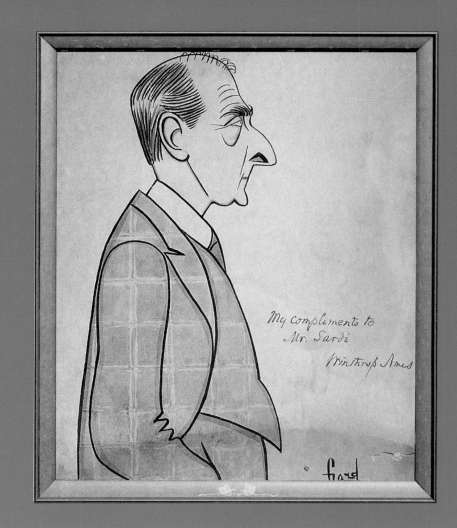

My compliments to Mr. Sardi
Winthrop Ames

in his assistant, director Guthrie McClintic, and the assistant's young actress bride, Katharine Cornell, to lunch. These three early patrons spread the word about the good food, cozy atmosphere and family feeling of the place. Before long, a pre-curtain crowd would include Walter Huston, Ed Wynn, Marie Dressler, Leslie Howard, H.L. Mencken, Sinclair Lewis, silent screen stars Lillian and Dorothy Gish, and all three Barrymores: John, Lionel and Ethel.

By 1926, we were part of a happily-ever-after, Horatio Alger success story. But not for long. Vincent Astor announced the demolition of our row of old brownstones, so that Abe Erlanger — of the powerful Klaw and Erlanger theater syndicate — could build a plush new playhouse on the site. Now, nobody hated Abe Erlanger as much as Lee and J.J. Shubert.

Lee Shubert, hearing of the plight of Sardi's, offered to build a three-story building for Mother and Dad down the block. The restaurant was to occupy the first and second floors;

THIS PAGE: SARDI'S SIDEWALK CAFÉ, WINTHROP AMES

14

a grand old dowager with startling blue eyes in old movies, but she was a magnificent leading lady in her time. Ethel Barrymore was the first actress of her generation to have a new Broadway playhouse named after her. The Shuberts built it in 1928, and were going to open it with Miss Barrymore herself starring in *The Kingdom of God*. Ethel took one look at the marquee on *her* theater, and flew in a rage toward Lee Shubert: "On the marquee, it states, 'MR. LEE SHUBERT PRESENTS ETHEL BARRYMORE IN THE KINGDOM OF GOD'." "So?" Lee shrugged. Barrymore huffed, "If it's *Mr.* Lee Shubert presenting, then *Mr.* Lee Shubert will present *Miss* Ethel Barrymore!"

Dad stood on the threshold of the new restaurant, flipping a twenty-dollar gold coin for luck. Mother chopped vegetables no one ate; their loyal waiter Carlo Oddone paced and cracked his knuckles; and vivacious, red-haired Renee Carroll, the hat-check girl, worked crossword puzzles behind her counter. Dad's gold coin turned into a silver dollar, then a quarter, and then a dime; but no one came.

the Shuberts would have their offices on the third floor, and there was to be a roof garden. We only had a short time to wait before our new home would be completed.

However, like other Shubert productions, the Shuberts' notion of a three-story building was not to be limited to the conventional three floors. J.J. wanted five floors, then Lee wanted seven, then J.J. *had* to have a palatial apartment on the top floor, which *had* to be higher than the apartment Lee had in the Sam S. Shubert theater across the street. Before they knew it, the building reached eleven stories.

By then, Mother and Dad had been out of the business a full year. The old regular crowd was long gone. The new Sardi's finally opened on March 5, 1927. I suppose the Shuberts felt guilty about the delay; instead of calling it "The Shubert Building," they christened it "The Sardi Building." It isn't often that anybody in show business voluntarily gives up billing on anything in favor of somebody else.

Well, take Ethel Barrymore. You probably remember her as

THIS PAGE: GUTHRIE McCLINTIC, VINCENT SARDI, SR. AND JENNY AT THE SARDI BUILDING.

FOLLOWING PAGE: DOUGLAS FAIRBANKS, JR., JANET GAYNOR, MIRIAM HOPKINS

To Alex.
Cheerio!
Douglas Fairbanks Jr.

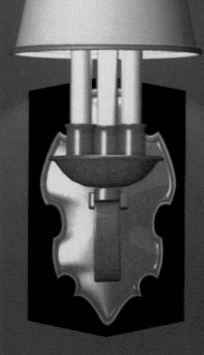

Janet Gaynor

Miriam Hopkins

"Cigarette me ~ Big Boy"
Ginger Rogers

Thank God! It
looks better to you
than it does to me
Raymond

Heigho Ho!
Rudy Vallée

Inspired by Mamoulian
Rouben Mamoulian
and raspberries
Jeanette MacDonald

Colby of *Variety*; and genial, rotund Kelcey Allen, drama critic of *Women's Wear Daily*.

Ring Lardner and Heywood Broun were defectors from the Algonquin to the Cheese Club, as well as Broadway columnists Walter Winchell, Louis Sobol and Mark Hellinger (who later became a film producer — the Hellinger theater on Broadway is named for him). Another frequent cheese was George Jessel, Winchell's former vaudeville partner. I'll wager you didn't know that Winchell was ever in vaudeville, but he and Jessel grew up on the same block and did a double singing act as kids.

The chief purpose of the Cheese Club was to keep its members amused, but now and then the members embarked on a more "humanitarian" cause. If some Cheeser took a liking to a young actor or, more likely, actress, that name would be dropped in members' columns, and poured into producers' ears. Needless to say, this largesse was often more than altruistic — although sometimes it was just a prank for a prank's sake. Irving Hoffman planted Renee Carroll's picture in the papers as

PREVIOUS PAGE: GINGER ROGERS, RAYMOND MASSEY, RUDY
VALLEE, JEANNETTE MacDONALD

THIS PAGE: THE INTERIOR OF SARDI'S IN THE 1920'S, THE
SARDI FAMILY AT A WEDDING DINNER, 1929

W hile Sardi's struggled, Broadway boomed. In the '27-'28 season alone, over two hundred and fifty productions opened in about sixty theaters — every thing from O'Neill's *Strange Interlude* to *Show Boat* to *Abie's Irish Rose*. Back in the 'twenties, New York also had fourteen daily newspapers, and each paper had its own staff of drama critics, Broadway columnists and caricaturists. And on top of that, each star and every show had its own press agent. Renee Carroll used to say, "Scratch a star and you'll find a press agent; scratch a press agent and he'll thank you."

Eventually, in 1927, a group of columnists and press agents started meeting at Sardi's every day for lunch. The Cheese Club, as they dubbed themselves, was dedicated to being less famous but more fun — and more spontaneous — than the "Round Table" at the Algonquin Hotel, where the wags of the "Vicious Circle" — George S. Kaufman, Dorothy Parker, Alexander Woollcott, et al. — wrote, rewrote, polished and rehearsed their famous "ad libs."

For the record, the chief cheeses of the club were cartoonist and columnist Harry Hershfield (a former Bartholdi Inn habitué); press agents Richard Maney, Nat Dorfman and Marc Lachman; reporters Sidney Skolsky, Whitney Bolton and Julius

a new Paramount Pictures starlet, and she had quite a few offers. Some of them were even on the up-and-up! Renee could handle them. Her motto was "steer clear of the ribbers, keep your nose clean and never mention 'Mammy' to Al Jolson."

Walter Winchell was Broadway's most powerful gossip columnist from 1928 to 1960, first for the *Evening Graphic* ("America's worst newspaper," according to Winchell), then for the New York *Daily Mirror* and on radio. Even his friends called him "ignorant, petty and vicious." Damon Runyon always said that Winchell never read a book in his life. "I have, too," Winchell replied, "I just can't remember the title." He maintained a life-long feud with the Shuberts, who banned him from all of their opening nights. That suited Winchell: "I can always go to the second night and see the closing."

Still, Winchell was capable of immense loyalty. He single-handedly kept Olsen and Johnson's *Hellzapoppin'* running almost forever, after every critic in town murdered it. And Winchell loved Sardi's. Even though he held court at the Stork Club, Winchell brought his wife and daughter to Sardi's two or three nights a week, and always plugged what he called "Mama and Papa Sardi's little fooderia" in his columns and on his radio show. Winchell's column was nationally syndicated in over a thousand papers. Millions of readers linked Sardi's with the stars.

One day, Irving Hoffman, a cartoonist as well as the press agent who fed Winchell most of his hot items, dragged a penniless Russian refugee named Alex Gard to sup with the Cheese Club. Born Alexis Kremkoff in Kazan, Russia, Gard had once been a cadet in the Russian Imperial Naval Academy, where he spent many a night in the brig for drawing satirical caricatures of his commanding officers. He spent World War I on a destroyer in the Baltic Sea, then fled Russia after the revolution. After a failed acting career in Bulgaria, Kremkoff landed without a franc in Paris. Calling himself "Garde" (as in *en garde*), he designed parade floats and occasionally published a caricature in *Le Matin*, where a typo shortened his *nom de plume* by a letter. The typo stuck for life.

Gard was a medium-sized man with darkish hair, strong features and a thick accent not unlike "The Mad Russian" on the old Eddie Cantor radio show. He had a habit of prefacing his sentences with "How d'you call it?" As he dined with the

THIS PAGE: ALEX GARD'S CONTRACT

FOLLOWING PAGE: GEORGE JESSEL, WALTER WINCHELL, LOUIS SOBOL, MARK HELLINGER, HEYWOOD BROUN, RING LARDNER

AGREEMENT

entered into this 19th day of September, 1927

between Alex Gard, herein after referred to as the party of the first part, and Vincent Sardi, herein after referred to as the part of the second part:

1. The party of the first part agrees to draw caricatures of well-known Broadway people who dine at Sardi's, the caricatures to cover the panels of the walls of the downstair's dining room.

2. The party of the second part agrees that in payment for the caricatures he will furnish the party of the first part with one meal per day, (beginning on the day this contract is signed, for the space of one year,) for himself and a guest, the meal to be either lunch or dinner to be chosen by the party of the first part.

3. The party of the second part agrees to pay for all materials used in making and framing the caricatures.

4. The party of the first part agrees that in the event he does not appear for either lunch or dinner on any one day he may not send a substitute, nor may he claim an extra meal on a following day.

5. It is agreed that the subjects of the caricatures referred to above must be agreed upon by both parties.

6. It is agreed that the party of the second part will not endeavor to rush the party of the first part in the completion of any one caricature, and on the other hand the party of the first part agrees to complete each caricature decided upon as promptly as compatible with his best standard of work.

7. The party of the first part agrees to draw caricatures which will be acceptable to the party of the first part, just as the party of the second part agrees to furnish meals which will be acceptable to the party of the first part.

SIGNED: *Alex Gard*
Party of the first part.

Date: *September 19, 1927*

Vincent Sardi
Party of the second part.

Witnessed:
Renée Carroll
Irving Hoffman

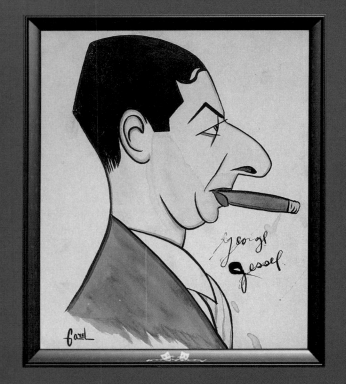

George Jessel.

DON BEVAN

Never again will I trust in Gurob.

Ring Around a Restaurant

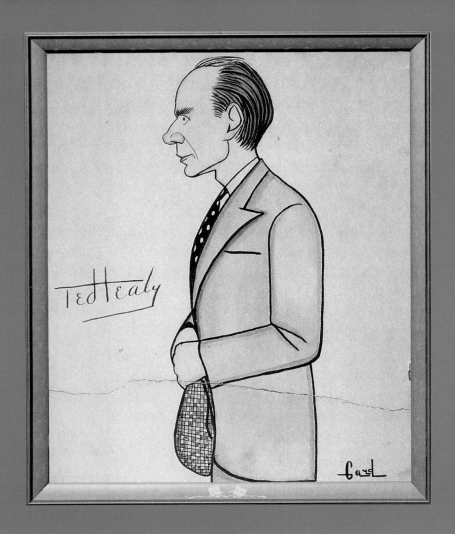

ment. Mr. Gard was to receive a meal a day in return for his caricatures. Dad was not permitted to complain about Mr. Gard's caricatures, and Gard was not allowed to complain about Mr. Sardi's food.

The first official Sardi's caricature was of Ted Healy, the bandleader and comedian only recalled today as the man who put the Three Stooges together. He's remembered at Sardi's for once bringing an orangutan to lunch. This was before he met Moe, Larry and Curly. The orangutan had better table manners than most of the Cheese Club. At various times, members brought their own menagerie of animals — including a cow and a sea lion — as publicity stunts. (The sea lion had an order of smelts.)

Producer Gene Buck once escorted a trained donkey to a press agents' luncheon on the second floor. "I've hired most of you jackasses at one time or another," Buck sputtered, "so I thought this time I'd do better with the real thing!" The donkey, a bib around his neck, seemed to enjoy himself until one of the

PREVIOUS PAGE: VINCENT PRICE, PETER LORRE, CHARLES COBURN, PAT O'BRIEN, LOUIS CALHERN

THIS PAGE: TED HEALY, LADY VIOLA TREE

Cheese Club, Gard dashed off caricatures of the members. Dad was so impressed and amused by Gard's caricatures that he posted them on the wall above the Cheese Club's table. Then the idea struck him. Dad recalled the tradition that had made Zelli's restaurant in Paris the favorite haunt of the French theater's matinee idols: the walls were covered with caricatures of the stars. Dad asked Gard if he'd like to try the Zelli experiment at Sardi's.

Gard, too, remembered Zelli's from his sojourn in Paris, and had ideas of his own. He wanted to choose his own subjects; he insisted that there be no changes to the drawings once he finished them; and he preferred to supply his own materials. Then the negotiations turned, as they will, to money. Dad, in his precarious financial state, hesitated to ask Gard how much money he wanted, but Gard wanted only a meal a day. Dad cheerfully agreed, but then Gard pulled Irving Hoffman aside. "How do I know this man's food vill be good?" Gard asked. "Maybe he vill cheat me to meals and give me bad food." Hoffman assured Gard that the food was excellent, but Gard wasn't mollified. He wanted something more formal.

And so, with Irving Hoffman and Renee Carroll as witnesses, Mr. Alex Gard and Mr. Vincent Sardi, Sr. signed a formal agree-

flacks fed him a chili pepper. On his way down the stairs, he knocked over a waiter who was carrying a tureen of soup, which went all over Buck and the press agents. After that, Renee Carroll tethered animals at the hat-check.

Gard started turning caricatures out by the dozens, and everyone wanted to be done. He soon became known as "the little man from Sardi's who puts big noses on big people." The Cheese Club helped him land a job as one of the regular theatrical caricaturists for the *New York Herald Tribune* (where he worked alongside a talented kid named Al Hirschfeld). By the time Gard drew a star for Sardi's gallery, he had already punctured his or her vanity several times over in the *Trib*.

Irving Hoffman once brought a member of a distinguished British acting dynasty, Lady Viola Tree, to Sardi's to join "Gard's Chosen People," only so that he could quip, "Only Gard can make a tree" (which is how her caricature was signed). But Gard couldn't be bought. The head of the New York Stock Exchange — who always ordered hot chocolate with his lunch and was called "Mr. Chocolate" by the waiters — wanted his

THIS PAGE: EDMUND GWENN, SYLVIA SIDNEY

mug on the wall. Gard said to the man's face, "You I wouldn't draw for ten thousand dollars."

Despite our family background, Sardi's has never been an Italian restaurant. We've always leaned more toward English food than any other style of cuisine. Back when Mother did most of the cooking, the food was, naturally, Italianesque. But Dad actually learned his side of the restaurant business in London, where he also learned to speak English. My sister Anne used to give him a hard time because he called Columbus Circle, "Columbus Circus."

With its warm paneling and soft lighting, the restaurant was designed to emulate a London club. Edmund Gwenn — the Welsh actor everyone remembers as Kris Kringle in *Miracle on 34th Street* — was attracted by the atmosphere, and always ordered broiled kidneys with Irish bacon and boiled Brussels sprouts — about as British a meal as you can find. (Gwenn was also one of the first actors to have Sardi's meals sent to his dressing room between shows on matinee days.)

Some of the regulars from Prohibition days like Sylvia Sidney say they remember Sardi's when it was a speakeasy, but it never was one. "21" was a speakeasy, and today, of course, "21"

is proud to have been a "speak." Bootleggers, rum-runners and speakeasies ruled the West Forties, and Mother and Dad could have made a small fortune selling bootleg hooch, but Dad wouldn't do it. He was a pretty stand-up, clean-cut guy, and he wouldn't break the law. Walter Winchell once wrote a long column about Dad, comparing him favorably to some of the other people in the restaurant business in New York.

Of course, that doesn't mean Mother and Dad didn't slip a snort to the regulars now and then. Mother would duck behind the cigar counter and come up with a "cup of coffee" that had been brewed in a bathtub over in Hell's Kitchen.

Occasionally, Gard would stray from the belters of Broadway like Sophie Tucker to another kind of belter: in this case, the "Manassa Mauler," Jack Dempsey. Even though the champ used to own his own restaurant, he courted his fourth wife in Sardi's. I guess wives number one, two and three wouldn't look for him there.

The provision that every cartoon had to be signed before it could be hung caused quite a few scenes. Helen Morgan — the unforgettable Julie of *Show Boat* — burst into tears when she saw her caricature and refused to sign her name to it. As you can see, she was persuaded to make an "X." Fannie Hurst, the novelist, hated her caricature, too. She thought that Gard had made her a tad too, shall we say, thick. But, being a good sport, she signed it anyway — then stewed for days. She came back and begged Gard to change it. Gard wouldn't budge. She got Winchell on the phone. Winchell told Dad that Miss Hurst wanted to buy her caricature. Dad told Winchell, "Well, the original belongs to Sardi's, and we don't sell them. But if she likes it so much, I might persuade Gard to make her a copy."

One of the first stage legends Gard caricatured was Katharine Cornell, whom he drew with a cigarette dangling from her mouth. Cornell refused to sign it until Gard removed the cigarette. Well, Alex Gard absolutely refused to change one of his drawings, *ever*, and Cornell stormed out of Sardi's, vowing never to return. Dad managed to get Gard to erase the offending butt. Then, he figured out a way to lure Cornell back with her favorite ingredient: garlic. Mother cooked up the "Katharine Cornell Salad:"

FACING PAGE: **SOPHIE TUCKER, JACK DEMPSEY, DAME JUDITH ANDERSON, TAMARA GEVA**

THIS PAGE: **HELEN MORGAN, FANNIE HURST**

FOLLOWING PAGE: **BARBARA STANWYCK, JOAN CRAWFORD**

Shred white cabbage the way you'd shred it for coleslaw. First, fry up some bacon till it's very crisp, remove it from the pan, and dry the grease out of it. Drain the skillet, then put in a tin of anchovy fillets and simmer them with a generous dollop of olive oil and a nice chunk of butter, and then add as much garlic as you want, minced or sliced thin. Let this cook over low heat until the anchovies are dissolved, then add two table spoons of vinegar or, better yet, fresh lemon juice. Then, put the shredded cabbage in a big salad bowl, and pour the hot anchovy-oil-butter-lemon dressing over it. Crumble the bacon over it all, toss it up, and serve it.

Cornell adored the salad, though she usually asked Mother to double the amount of garlic in her order. Once, while Cornell was appearing on Broadway, her co-star would call up nightly to see if Miss Cornell had ordered "her" salad — so that he could eat garlic himself that night. Eventually, we had to take the "Cornell Salad" off the menu: too many patrons complained about the amount of garlic.

One of Eli Wallach's first breaks was as a spear-carrier to Cornell's Queen of the Nile in Shakespeare's *Antony and Cleopatra*. He had a short speech informing Cleo that Tony had married Octavia. Wallach was supposed to stand there until Cornell finished a string of long speeches. Now, according to Lee Strasberg's "method," which Eli was studying at the time, when an actor comes on stage to do something, he's never supposed to just stand there. "I kept interrupting her," Eli explained to Strasberg, "to make my presence real. 'Madam …' And she'd keep talking, and then I'd say, 'Madam!' And she'd keep talking, and it all seemed very real, but the third time I said 'MADAM!' she hauled off and hit me! What did I do wrong?" "Idiot!" Strasberg snapped. "What the hell kind of Method is that? Wait for your goddamn cues!"

Lee Strasberg, Cheryl Crawford and Harold Clurman were the founders of the Group Theater. Crawford — who later produced B*rigadoon* and *The Rose Tattoo* — called them "a bizarre trio, two Old Testament prophets and a *shiksa*." They were

PREVIOUS PAGE: **BETTE DAVIS, KATHARINE CORNELL**

THIS PAGE: **HAROLD CLURMAN, CHERYL CRAWFORD, LEE STRASBERG**

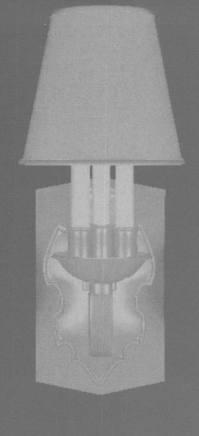

young, leftist and working for the Theater Guild. Stanislavski's Moscow Art Theater had visited Broadway in the 1920's, and the Group wanted to emulate the honesty and psychological complexity of the Russian company's ensemble acting. The Group Theater's acting ranks included Jules (later John) Garfield, Morris Carnovsky, Franchot Tone, Sanford Meisner, Frances Farmer, Lee J. Cobb, Robert "Bobby" Lewis and playwright Clifford Odets.

There were no stars in the Group. They were all "working actors," but two of those working actors had noble blood: Stella Adler and her brother Luther were the offspring of the one and only Jacob Adler, the "King" of the Yiddish Theater. The Yiddish Theater's influence on American acting is never really given its due. There were more than twenty Yiddish-language theaters down around the Bowery and Second Avenue in the 'twenties. Clurman called its acting style "realism with a little

extra." There was a lot of claptrap, to be sure, but there was wonderful acting and there were big stars, many of whom "crossed over" to Broadway, like Molly Picon and Menasha Skulnick.

Ironically, one of the favorite plays of the Yiddish Theater was King Lear, transformed into the tale of an aged merchant on the Lower East Side dividing the family business among his greedy children. Lee J. Cobb — the original Willy Loman in Death of a Salesman whose real name was Leo Jacob — was playing Shakespeare's Lear at Lincoln Center in the 'sixties. Cobb was taking a taxi to the theater, and the driver was an old guy who'd been raised on the Lower East Side. "What play are you in?" asked the cabbie. Cobb said he was doing King Lear. The cabbie got a nostalgic gleam in his eyes. "Ahhhh, King Lear! Tell me, is it any good in English?"

Muni Weisenfreund also started in the Yiddish Theater. You'd know him as Paul Muni. He played a sixty-year-old man at the age of twelve in 1908, and acted only in Yiddish through 1926, always playing old men. He wanted to leave Second Avenue for Broadway, but he couldn't get anyone to take him seriously. Then he heard that Sam Harris — who was a "name" producer — was hunting for somebody to replace Edward G.

THIS PAGE: STELLA ADLER, MOLLY PICON

FOLLOWING PAGE: MAURICE CHEVALIER, HERMIONE GINGOLD, MENASHA SKULNICK, CELESTE HOLM

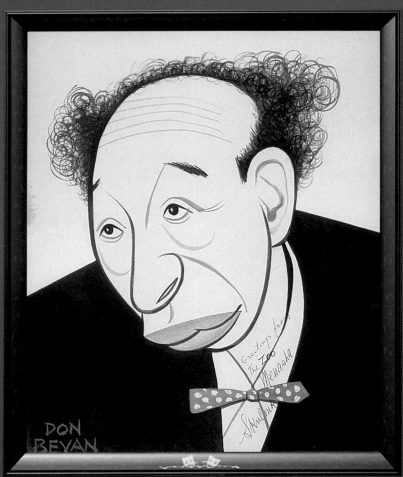

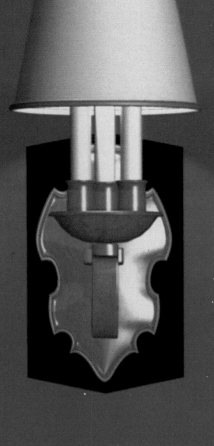

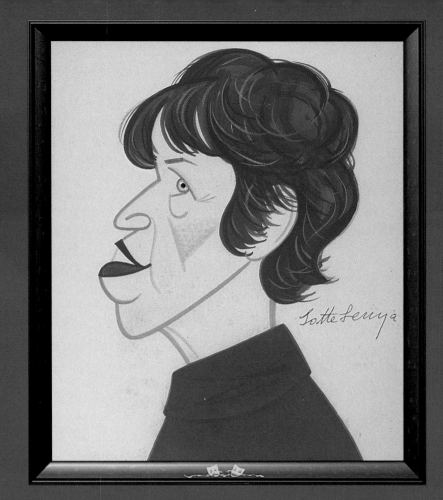
Lotte Lenya

Beatrice Lillie

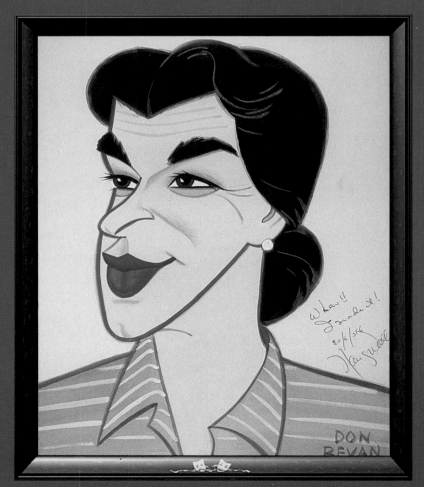
DON BEVAN

Robinson, who was playing an old man. Muni knew he could play the role to perfection, so he tracked Sam Harris to Sardi's, and presented himself at Sam's table.

Harris exploded at Muni: "I don't need any wet-behind-the-ears kids. I need some old geezer, one of those suckers who used to work for me in the old days. Get out!" Sam Harris dug back into his spaghetti, and he heard this grizzled voice from the next table. "You're right, Sam. We old bastards shouldn't let any of them young punks into the theater. What do they know? Still wet in the diapers." Harris turned his head and saw Paul Muni sitting there, grinning. Muni got the part.

You remember Reno Sweeney in *Anything Goes*, the Ethel Merman character, who was inexplicably an evangelist and a night-club singer? Well, Reno Sweeney was a send-up of Texas Guinan. Texas started out in hundreds of two-reel westerns. "We never changed the plots," she said, "only the horses." But she made her name as "The Queen of the Night Clubs" — in fact, when she starred in a very early talkie of the same name, she was so loyal to Sardi's that she had Warner Brothers hire Alex Gard to design the posters and lobby cards. She always greeted her fans with her catchphrase, "Hello, suckers!",

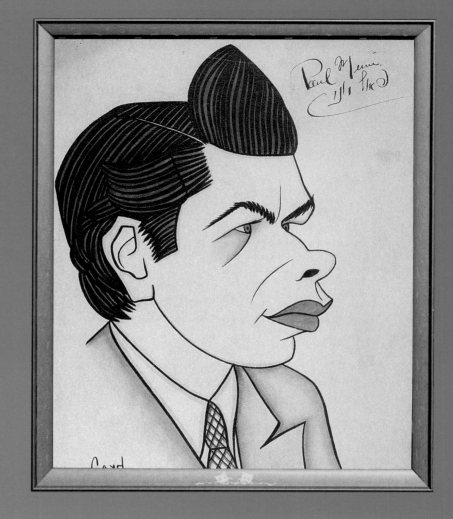

signed autographs with her thumbprint and lived with her parents — and an occasional gangster or two — in a bizarrely decorated apartment in the Village. The windows were painted black in defiance of sunrise. The Feds raided and padlocked so many of Tex's clandestine clubs that she wore a necklace made of tiny gold-plated locks, each engraved with the name of one of her nightclubs. The Prince of Wales (long before he met Wallis Warfield Simpson) was once caught in a raid. Texas hustled H.R.H. into the kitchen, handed him a chef's hat and ordered the once and future King of England to "keep fryin' eggs till the coast is clear!"

The Shuberts starred Texas in the raucous revue *Padlocks of 1927*, where her curtain line to the departing audience was, "Now go and eat at Sardi's, suckers!" Texas and several of her

PREVIOUS PAGE: LOTTE LENYA, BEATRICE LILLIE, NANCY WALKER
THIS PAGE: LEE J. COBB, PAUL MUNI

32

club's doorman gunned him down in '29.

About that time a couple of mobsters tried to pull a protection racket on Sardi's, with the line, "We wanna have a look at your beer pipes — to see if they need fixin'." Now, Dad didn't have any beer pipes, of course, and when Texas heard about this little shakedown, she and Larry Fay went to have a little talk with the "boys." A couple of days later, the same gangsters came back into Sardi's. The thugs politely asked for a table and behaved themselves. They informed Dad, "Texas told us to mind our manners!"

Now, about the Reno Sweeney part. In 1933, Texas was "converted" by Aimee Semple MacPherson, the tent-show evangelist, and from then on she considered her night-club performances her own form of preaching. She'd say, "Aimee goes in for saving souls; I go in for saving heels." She died later that year, exactly one month before Prohibition was repealed.

chorus girls used to tool up to Sardi's at four o'clock in the afternoon — for breakfast — in an armored car with bullet-proof tires that once belonged to the King of Belgium.

She had a real eye for talent in picking her chorines. Ruby Keeler started out in the line, went out to Hollywood a chorus girl and came back a star (and married Al Jolson). Another Ruby in the chorus, Ruby Stevens, born in Brooklyn and orphaned at the age of four, landed a big role in the play *Burlesque* and then headed to tinseltown herself. Between 1930 and 1939 she made no less than thirty-four movies, as Barbara Stanwyck.

Texas Guinan's bosom buddy was Public Enemy Number Three Larry Fay (Dillinger was Number One). Even though Fay had little quirks like painting his fingernails bright red, he was certainly nobody to mess with — at least until his own night-

THIS PAGE: SAM HARRIS, TEXAS GUINAN

FOLLOWING PAGE: BERT LAHR, RAY BOLGER

33

Thanks!
(after 60 years it's
high-time)" With
special love also!
Maggie Hamilton

K. Barat

Greetings?
Frank Morgan

Card

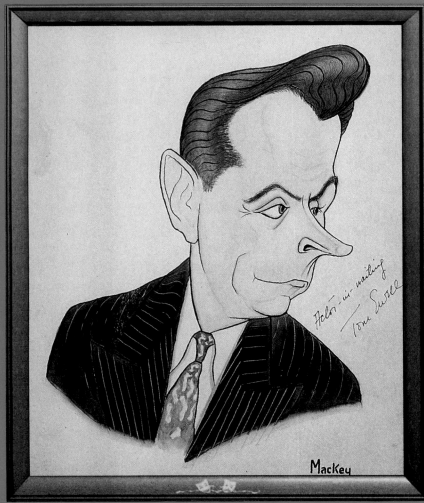

Mother and Dad commemorated the Twenty-First Amendment by opening the very smallest bar in New York, called, fittingly enough, "The Little Bar." My parents always treated the restaurant as their own home, and expected the patrons, famous or not, to stay sober and behave as if they were guests of the family. Dad condoned drinking, but not to excess. He wouldn't allow any boisterousness or vulgarity. He hated to see regulars getting loaded. He'd put on his overcoat, turn the restaurant over to the head waiter, and go out for a walk.

He'd never take advantage of the presence of stars. He always said, "They're entitled to eat in peace and quiet, too." In fact, that was one of the secrets of Sardi's. Dad always treated celebrities just like ordinary people and ordinary people like celebrities.

"The Little Bar" developed its own circle of regulars, who staked out the territory and defended it fiercely. It was shaped like a half-moon, so a crasher had to interrupt a conversation just to reach the bar. In the 'forties and 'fifties "The Little Bar" club was made up of Broadway actors like Tom Ewell, David Wayne (whose caricature was done by Gard during the run of *Finian's Rainbow* in which Wayne played a leprechaun, hence the sketch of the pointed ears), character man Philip Coolidge, and charter members from Hollywood Rex Harrison, John Carradine and Melville Cooper.

The boys at "The Little Bar" could be cruel to outsiders. Robert Preston, a ringleader of the fraternity, used to tell a story about that immensely gifted actor Rod Steiger. Steiger, it seems, had a pathological fear of mingling with other actors, yet longed to be a part of the "inner circle" at "The Little Bar." After years with his therapist, Steiger finally thought he was ready to join in. One fine day he screwed his courage to the sticking place, strode into "The Little Bar," elbowed his way in, smiled broadly at the regulars, and said to the bartender, "I'll have a Scotch." "Scotch and what?" asked the bartender. Steiger faltered. He hadn't rehearsed another line. "Let's see …" he stammered, "I dunno, I, I, I guess a ginger ale." All heads at the bar turned, and the regulars all said as one, "A GINGER ALE?" Steiger fled. Rod Steiger did come into the restaurant again, and our beloved long-time *maitre d'*, Jimmy Molinsky, and I appeared (as ourselves) in a movie with him called *No Way To Treat A Lady*.

PREVIOUS PAGE: MARGARET HAMILTON, FRANK MORGAN

THIS PAGE: "THE LITTLE BAR," TOM EWELL

FACING PAGE: ROBERT PRESTON, DAVID WAYNE,
                              REX HARRISON

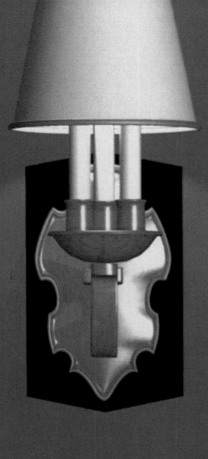

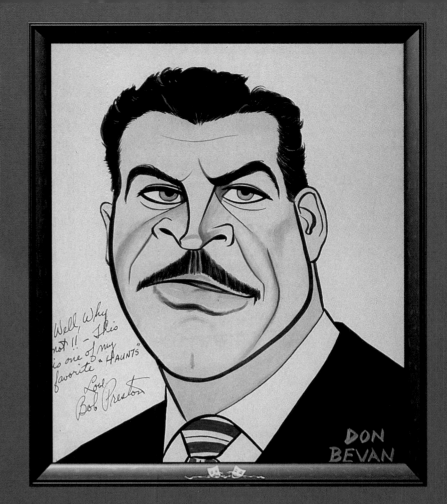

Well Why
not !! - This
is one of my
favorite "HAUNTS"
Lou
Bob Preston

DON
BEVAN

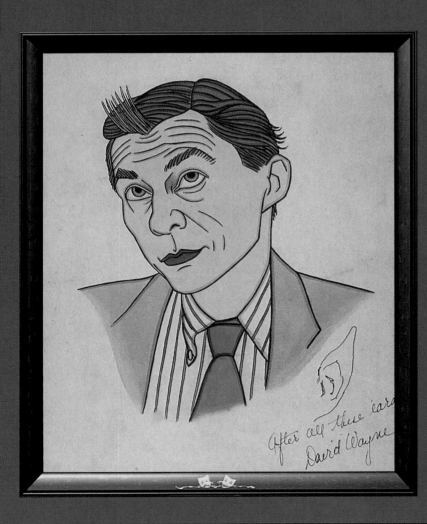

After all these years
David Wayne

Henry "Rex"
Harrison.

MacKey

very first Antoinette Perry award as Cyrano.

By the way, if you look closely at Jose Ferrer's caricature, you'll see the only likeness of Alex Gard in Sardi's. Ferrer, an artist himself, drew a caricature of Alex Gard next to his autograph.

Speaking of noses, do you recognize the fellow in profile here with the rather Cyrano-like schnozz? I'd be surprised if you did. It's "Uncle Miltie" — Milton Berle. Gard drew Berle back when he was appearing in vaudeville and revues. When Berle saw himself on Sardi's walls, he went right out and got a nose job. The moment the bandages came off, Berle went up to Gard and demanded that a new caricature — with the new nose — be done at once. Gard never re-drew a caricature, but he did offer to draw a dotted line along the old nose, indicating where Berle's new nose was. The matter was dropped.

Even though Dad generally clucked his tongue at heavy drinkers, he did welcome some of the theater's legendary tipplers. Everybody in the theater has a Tallulah Bankhead

THIS PAGE: **JOSÉ FERRER, FERRER AS CYRANO DE BERGERAC**

There's a photograph, not a caricature, hanging in "The Little Bar" of José Ferrer as Cyrano de Bergerac, its frame extended to accommodate Cyrano's monstrous nose. Jimmy Durante came into the bar once, looked at Ferrer's prosthetic proboscis, and cried, "That man's an impostor!" Ferrer claims he never would have played Cyrano at all if it hadn't been for Dad. During a "dry spell" on its way to being a drought in his career, Dad allowed Ferrer to keep running a tab, and never once asked for payment. One day, however, Ferrer asked Dad for a total, and was told the amount he owed was upwards of twelve hundred dollars — quite a bundle in those days. Ferrer was determined to pay the debt.

He couldn't seem to land a role in anybody else's production, so he thought he'd try producing himself. The first script he picked up was none other than *Cyrano de Bergerac*, and the rest, as they say, is show business history. Some years ago the person responsible for taking care of the caricatures was a Puerto Rican busboy. His job was to take them down, wash the glass, dust the frames, and put them back up again. He always took special pains with José Ferrer's image under glass. Like the busboy, Ferrer was from Puerto Rico, arrived here without a cent, unable to speak English — and he won an Oscar and the

story, and I'm sure most of them are true. "Tallulah's always skating on thin ice," quipped Shaw's first Eliza Doolittle, Mrs. Patrick Campbell, "and everyone wants to be there when it breaks." Once Tallulah was in the ladies' restroom upstairs and ran out of toilet tissue. Tallulah said to the woman in the next stall, "Dahling, do you have any paper in there?" The woman said no, so Tallulah said, "In that case, do you have two fives for a ten?"

In the middle of a performance, if Tallulah thought the proceedings had become a little dull, she was wont to turn cartwheels to keep the audience awake. Perhaps that's why nobody in New York really took her seriously as an actress until she played Regina in Lillian Hellman's *The Little Foxes* in 1939. Her father was an Alabama congressman (later Speaker of the House), so Tallulah knew all about Southern politics and "steel magnolias." Bankhead's feud with Hellman became a press agent's dream. Tallulah: "Lillian knows so much, she really does; but she thinks she knows just a little bit more than she really does." Hellman on Bankhead: "Tallulah is a very good actress,

THIS PAGE: MILTON BERLE, TALLULAH BANKHEAD

FOLLOWING PAGE: BURGESS MEREDITH, JACKIE COOPER,
                     KARL MALDEN, DAN DAILEY, LLOYD NOLAN

but she is also the biggest bore God ever created." Bankhead's retort: "I say she's spinach and the Hellman with her."

Bette Davis played Bankhead's role in William Wyler's film of *The Little Foxes* as well as Tallulah's stage roles in *Jezebel* and *Dark Victory*. Tallulah ran into Davis in Sardi's years later and croaked, "Bette, dahhhh-ling, I played them all much better than you did." All Davis said was, "I agree." Tallulah's favorite order at Sardi's? A bowl of Vichyssoise and four daiquiris.

Dad always looked out for young actors and actresses. He never encouraged them to spend a lot of money. He'd volunteer his own brand of loan or credit; but often he took a tougher stance. If an actor came in needing a shave or in rumpled clothes, he'd ask, "How do you expect to get a part looking like that? How will you look to a producer?" He'd hand the actor a dollar or two, and order him to "get a haircut … get a shave … press your suit. Come in smiling … look like something!"

Some actors couldn't save money even when they had good paying jobs. They'd bring Dad half of their pay checks; he'd dole out a small allowance, then he'd open a savings account in the actor's name, which became known as the "Sardi Bank and Trust Company." Dad helped them salt away quite a little slush fund.

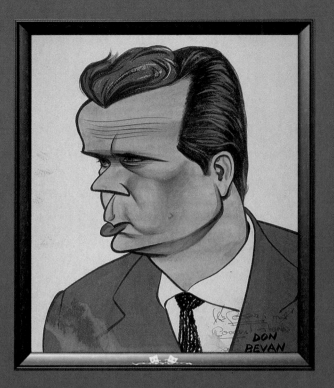

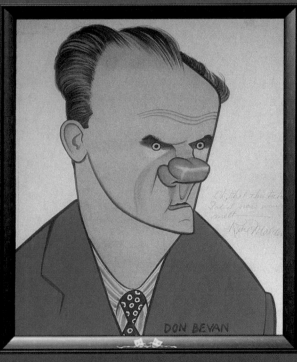

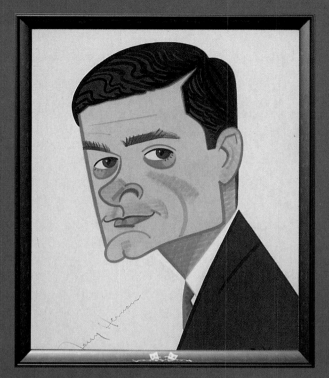

— his favorite brother Domenico back in Italy was an actor — even though the rest of the family considered Domenico the "black sheep." They wanted him to become a priest. Though Mother never gave acting a second thought after she married Dad, he himself played a captain of waiters in a silent movie called *The Worst Woman In Town*.

They shot in a studio in the Bronx, where Mom and Dad were living at the time. After the shoot, Mother invited the whole cast and crew back to their apartment for a party. Mother and Dad thought they'd bought too much food, until the locusts arrived. By the time the party was over, there wasn't a crumb. Dad had happily spent twice his salary from the picture on the party! His role in the movie, alas, ended up on the cutting room floor.

It looked for a while like I was going to be the actor of the family. Winthrop Ames and the actors Wallace Ford and Frank

PREVIOUS PAGE: ABE BURROWS, JERRY HERMAN,
                   JEROME ROBBINS, MICHAEL BENNETT,
                   TOMMY TUNE

THIS PAGE: PROGRAM FROM "THE MASTER OF THE INN"
                   PROGRAM FROM "BRIGHT LIGHTS OF 1944"

Dad was a soft touch for the legitimate person in need, but he never loaned money in a conventional sense. When he gave you cash, it was a gift. He never expected to see it again. In the early days, I figure he sustained at least $3,500 a year in losses on actor meals alone — and that was a lot more in those days than it is now! Still, Dad was wary of the professional borrower. If someone came in wanting to see "Vincent," that was a sure tip-off that he was there for a scam. Everyone — even good friends and regular customers — always called Dad "Mr. Sardi." Dad's devotion to his clients was immense. He never forgot anyone's birthday; when producers had shows in trouble, Dad often sent over checks to help them meet payroll.

When I took over the restaurant, I found a three-foot-long drawer in his desk full of unpaid tabs that went back to the 'twenties. He'd just forgotten about them. After he retired, he wrote, "According to the popular view, actors are people who live in another world. They are not like the rest of us. They are artistic — and because they are, they are irrepressible, irresponsible, and, most of the time, broke. This is the popular conception. It isn't mine. If it were true, I would have gone bankrupt!"

From an early age, Dad was always partial to "show people"

42

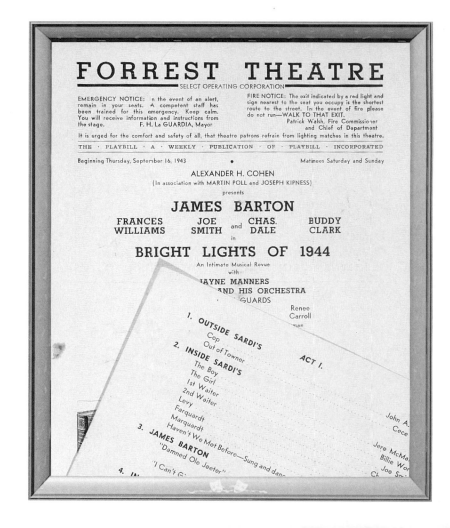

Craven persuaded Dad to let me make my stage debut in a play called *The Master of the Inn*. When it previewed at the Lyric Theater in Allentown, Pennsylvania, I was billed as "Vincent Serdi." To give you some idea of the times, I was playing a character called "Pietro, the little Wop." At one moment in the play, my exit line was "Adios," and I told the director that it really should have been "Addio." He snapped at me, "You play it exactly as written." The play opened at Ames's Little Theater in 1925, and after that, I appeared in two other plays, *Send No Money* and *Buckaroo*, in which Renee Carroll, the Sardi's hatcheck girl, also appeared. The reviews on *Buckaroo* were so bad that the producers cut out all the extras right after opening night, including Renee and me.

More recently, my acting has been confined to playing myself whenever a movie has been filmed in Sardi's. In fact, I've played myself so often that I'm a member of the Screen Actors Guild. You may remember the scene where Liza Minnelli had me throw Kermit the Frog out of the restaurant in *The Muppets Take Manhattan*. Kermit tried to steal Liza's caricature

THIS PAGE: CHARLES NELSON REILLY, KERMIT THE FROG

FOLLOWING PAGE: SIR MICHAEL REDGRAVE, SIR JOHN MILLS, SIR ANTHONY QUAYLE

and put his own up on the wall to boost his theatrical career. Some of the other films shot in Sardi's were *No Way To Treat A Lady* with Rod Steiger; *Made For Each Other* in 1971; *Please Don't Eat the Daisies* with Doris Day and David Niven playing thinly disguised versions of Jean and Walter Kerr (and based on Jean's book); *The Fan* with Lauren Bacall; and Martin Scorsese's *King Of Comedy*.

In the last film, our caricaturist Richard Baratz can be seen drawing the caricature of Robert DeNiro that hangs on the wall. You know that DeNiro goes to great lengths to make all his characters convincing. Well, when it came time for DeNiro to sign his name, he signed it as "Rupert Pupkin," the name of his character in the movie.

Not only have movie companies used the real Sardi's, but in *Critic's Choice* with Bob Hope and Lucille Ball (yet another *film a clef* about the Kerrs) and a couple of other films, they've recreated the restaurant on soundstages in Hollywood. We've sent plates, menus, and other "Sardibilia" to make the props more authentic.

Sardi's itself did finally make it to Broadway. Smith and Dale, the old vaudeville team that inspired Neil Simon's *The Sunshine Boys*, did a Broadway revue called *Bright Lights of 1944*.

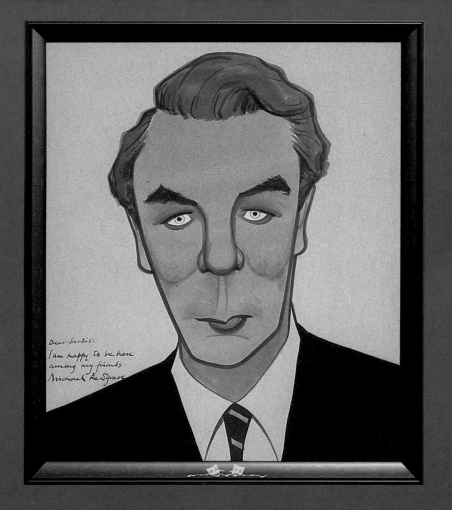

Dear Sardi's:
I am happy to be here
among my friends
Michael Redgrave

It took patience + fortitude, but thank Gard, I made it.

It was set in Sardi's. Darryl Hickman and Charles Nelson Reilly spent weeks in the 'seventies interviewing Dad for a musical they were doing about the early days of the restaurant. Charles was the director, Darryl the bookwriter and Michel Legrand was to compose the score. Sergio Franchi had committed to play Dad and Anna Maria Alberghetti was to play Mother, but like so many good ideas, it never happened.

It wasn't the first time Dad was involved in getting a show off the ground. In the early days, one penniless would-be producer had lined up a potential backer for lunch. He persuaded Dad to lend him a hundred dollars, so that he could wine and dine the man. Dad cleaned out the till and made him the loan. The producer came in, asked for the best table, and tipped Dad twenty dollars — of Dad's own money!

Will Morrissey was known as a "cuff producer" — which meant that he went into production without enough money to pay for the show — he produced "off the cuff." Morrissey was trying to raise some cash for a revue starring Milton Berle he already had in rehearsal. He brought a rich Texas oil man into Sardi's and told him all about the show he was going to put his cash into. It looked like the Texan was going to fork over, until he asked Morrissey for a script.

Well, Morrissey didn't have one. In fact, the show was being written in rehearsal. Still, he didn't want to let a live one off the hook, so Morrissey dashed to the hat-check stand, and asked Renee Carroll for a script — any script. The first manuscript she put her hands on was a copy of Eugene O'Neill's *Strange Interlude*. Morrissey handed the Texan the six-hour Freudian gloomfest and sent him away — after collecting a check. A couple of weeks later, the Texan "angel" dropped by rehearsal and saw Berle, dog acts and chorus girls. He wanted to know why the show was so different from the script. "Well," Morrissey shrugged,"you know how they're always changing things in rehearsal!"

Dad made it a policy never to invest in shows. But Renee Carroll made quite a bit of cash for herself as a backer. Often, producers would check scripts with their coats and hats. By the time they reclaimed their belongings, Renee had read the play and decided whether or not to back their shows. When she left Sardi's, she owned a half interest in a ticket agency (and married its owner, the "Mayor of 44th Street," Lou Schon-

PREVIOUS PAGE: **GLYNIS JOHNS, PAUL SCOFIELD, PETER USTINOV, MARGARET LEIGHTON**

THIS PAGE: **RENEE CARROLL, ERNST LUBITSCH**

ceit), lots of real estate, and shares in several long-running hits. She must be the only hat-check girl ever to publish her memoirs, *In Your Hat*, published in 1933 and illustrated by — who else? — Alex Gard.

Gangster Arnold Rothstein once offered Renee a thousand-dollar tip for his hat. She refused. Yet she chewed out Maurice Chevalier for leaving his trademark straw boater in his car to cheat Renee out of a dime. "Maurice Chevalier eats so much fish," Renee said, "he smells like Gloucester, Mass." Wisecracks were part of her stock-in-trade. She once told the Shuberts' press agent, "You're so loud you make a racket buttoning your over coat." The great musical star Gertrude Lawrence admired Renee's Woolworth pearls, and offered to give Renee her autograph in exchange for them. "No dice," snapped Renee; Gertie gave Renee her autograph anyway.

Back in the 'twenties, Mother and Dad started to have as many film people in here as we did theater people. Greta Garbo sent word that she would be having her luncheon at Sardi's. When she arrived, she was preceded by fifteen bodyguards, who swarmed in, requesting patrons not to demand autographs. When Garbo herself arrived, no one even turned a head.

When the talkies hit, studios were desperate for actors who could actually speak their lines. Broadway was their natural hunting ground, and many fine stage actors were lured away to Hollywood. During the silent days, most of the studios had main offices in midtown. Each studio had its own table at Sardi's. There was a Paramount table, an MGM table, and so forth. With the advent of the talkies, production moved to the coast. A lot of Dad's business went with it.

A lot of kids knocking around Broadway in those days became big stars in Hollywood. Jimmy Cagney was working as a chorus boy when he started coming in here. There were many days when all he had to eat was a bowl of soup at Sardi's — on credit. Once he hit it big, he never forgot how kind Dad was to him. Not long before he died, he was in New York shooting his last movie — some made-for-TV drama — and came in for lunch. Nobody bothered him until he got up to leave. Then the entire place rose to its feet and gave him one of his last ovations. It wasn't long after he died that someone stole his caricature.

Many regulars now exiled to the Coast wrote back and

THIS PAGE: **FRITZ LANG, LUIGI PIRANDELLO**

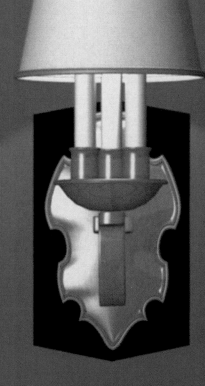

begged Dad to close up shop in New York and move to Los Angeles. Add this inducement to the Stock Market Crash, and you'll understand why Dad seriously considered it. But Mother was adamant: 44th Street is our home, and I don't want to leave it." By the way, in the '29 Crash, it's rumored that Lee Shubert lost over ten million dollars. "My only consolation," he joked, "is that my brother J.J. gets fifty percent."

The Brown Derby offered Alex Gard a huge salary to make the move and do his caricatures for them. Fortunately for Sardi's, Alex hated everything L.A. stood for. In his own words, "I hate Hollywood. There wasn't a single day when I didn't run into at least two or three characters I had seen years back in New York. On Broadway they were trying to chisel a couple of dollars around the theaters; in Hollywood they are rich and influential, although many of them wouldn't be able to describe their connection with the picture industry." Alex finally made the sojourn in the 'forties in order to do a book of Hollywood stars. They turned out anything but glamorous. Maybe he always harbored a grudge for what Hollywood did to business at Sardi's.

Dad's business didn't really improve until 1938, when the shift in fortune can be attributed to one man: Maurice Evans. Today, if anyone remembers Maurice Evans, it's either as the chief orangutan in *Planet of the Apes*, or as Elizabeth Montgomery's warlock father on the old *Bewitched* TV series. At the time, however, Evans was a huge box office draw, in Shakespeare, no less. In 1938, Evans and director Margaret Webster planned a Broadway production of *Hamlet*. Now, there had been many Hamlets on the Broadway stage before, from John Barrymore's in 1924 to the 1936-37 season, when John Gielgud and Leslie Howard *both* took the "Sweet Prince" to Broadway.

But Evans was a Dane with a difference; for the first time in the commercial theater, he and Webster were going to present the play uncut, in its entirety. The curtain at the St. James went up at 6:30 p.m., and came down after 10:30. The performance was bisected by a dinner break (not unlike the eight-and-a-half-hour marathon *Nicholas Nickleby* decades later). Prominently displayed in the program was a notice from Mr. Evans urging patrons to dine at Sardi's! Mother and Dad fixed a special

FACING PAGE: MAURICE EVANS, LESLIE HOWARD, SIR JOHN GIELGUD

THIS PAGE: SARDI'S MENUS, VINCENT SARDI, SR. AT WORK

FOLLOWING PAGE: EDWARD ANDREWS, FRED CLARK, JAMES COCO, LOU JACOBI, JACK GILFORD, HERSCHEL BERNARDI

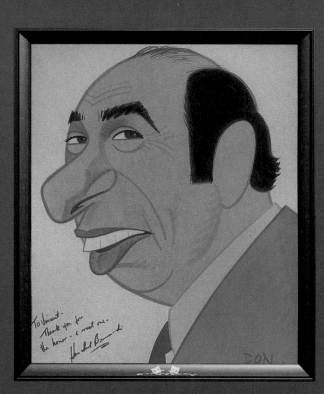

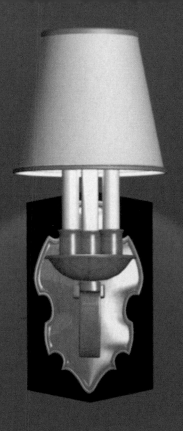

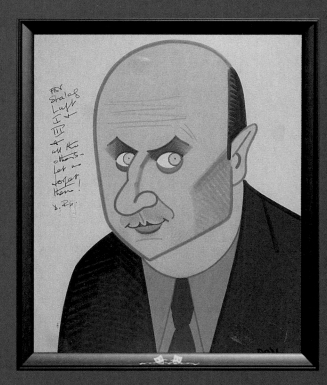

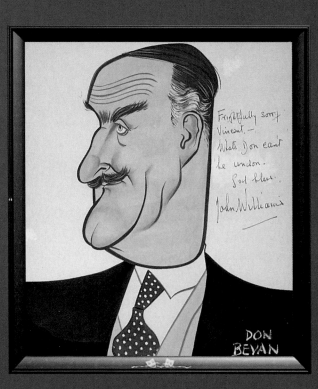

"Hamlet Supper," guaranteeing to get the audience back to the St. James in time for poor Yorick.

As a matter of fact, in the New York *Herald Tribune* Lucius Beebe invoked the shade of Hamlet when he praised Dad's contribution to the drama: "Vincent Sardi is probably responsible for any number of great stage performances. The genius of actors is notoriously integrated to their digestions. A properly aerated cheese soufflé or a turtle soup with just the right amount of amontillado may make the difference between a stumblebum Dane and a Hamlet of John Gielgudian proportions."

Dad was always out front; everyone knew him and identified him with the restaurant. Behind the scenes, keeping it all running, was Mother. Mother would get up in the morning, prepare breakfast for my sister and me, and then she'd take the train from Flushing into Penn Station. Rain, snow, or shine, she'd walk up to 44th Street, to save a nickel on the subway. By 7:30 a.m., she'd have ordered all the food. She supervised the kitchen and all the preparation, which we call the *mise en place*. When the food arrived, she'd check it all, make sure that it all arrived, then oversee the prep. Once the meals were being cooked, she'd take her place at the cigar counter and take the cash. When Dad retired, I took his place; when Mother retired, I had to hire four or five people to replace her.

Dad drove in around eleven, ran the dining room for lunch, then headed to the office for a round of paperwork. In the afternoon, he'd go to the Trans-Lux, a movie theater that exclusively showed newsreels. He was, in fact, interested in current events, but more often than not, he went there for a short nap. He'd come back refreshed for the pre-theater dinner trade. While Mother took the train back to Flushing, Dad would stay and close the restaurant at one in the morning, when he'd drive back to Flushing. My parents worked awfully hard, but I'd never call them workaholics. When you're that busy and you love what you're doing, you never know where the time goes.

Dad left home when he was twelve; he didn't have much formal education, yet he was probably one of the best educated men I've known. There were a lot of newspapers in those

PREVIOUS PAGE: **CYRIL RITCHARD, DONALD PLEASENCE, STANLEY HOLLOWAY, WILFRID HYDE-WHITE, JOHN WILLIAMS**

THIS PAGE: **EUGENIA, VINCENT, JR. AND VINCENT SARDI, SR. AT THE CIGAR COUNTER**

days, and Dad read them all. Whenever he had time, he'd read, read, read. When I was going to Columbia, my classmates would come home with me. Before I'd know it, they'd be in debates with Dad. You could never win with him, either, because he always had the FACTS.

John Golden, the very influential producer whose name endows one of our best small Broadway houses, came into Sardi's almost every day for lunch, often in the company of such notables as Eleanor Roosevelt, Mary Lasker or Bernard Baruch. Instead of sitting at one of the front tables with the other celebrities, Mr. Golden absolutely insisted on sitting next to the cigar counter. Once Dad strongly urged him to move to a much more prominent table near the front, but Golden protested, "How can I see your wife's hair from there?" Mother had the most beautiful silver-white hair. He also adamantly refused to be caricatured, but we still have a plaque commemorating "John Golden's Table."

During my Columbia days I worked behind the cigar counter on Saturdays. I'd actually managed to flunk a couple of subjects. Dad said the cigar counter was a job; I thought it was punishment. But that's when I really started to get to know the restaurant. As time went by, Dad and Mother took out the cigar counter, and I started acting as the host in the second floor dining room. It wasn't so much that I discovered a passion for the restaurant business; I just fell in love with Sardi's. I switched my major at Columbia from pre-med to business administration.

After graduation, Dad sent me to apprentice with Louis Diat at the Ritz for two years in his kitchen, where I learned plenty. When Dad officially brought me into the restaurant, he had me doing everything, buying produce, waiting on tables, making cost analyses, everything. When I was done serving the pre-theater crowd, I'd dash off to the opera or theater myself. This was back when the old Metropolitan Opera House was in midtown. I'd change from tux into white tie and hustle to the Met.

One time, when I was sharing a box with my sister and brother-in-law, the couple sitting next to me stared at me through the whole first act. When the house lights went up, they looked at me with amazement, then disdain. You see, I'd served them their dinners not half an hour before.

THIS PAGE: VINCENT, JR., EUGENIA AND VINCENT SARDI, SR.

FOLLOWING PAGE: RUTH GORDON, GARSON KANIN, ELI WALLACH, ANNE JACKSON

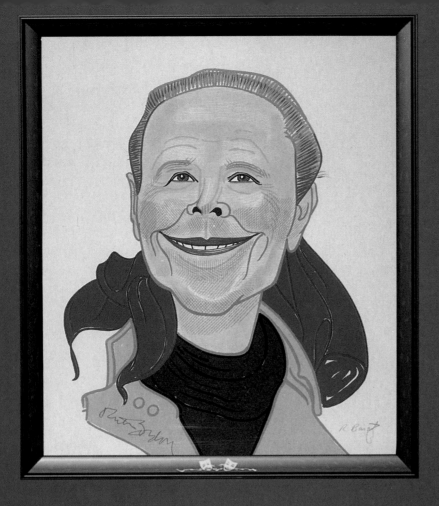
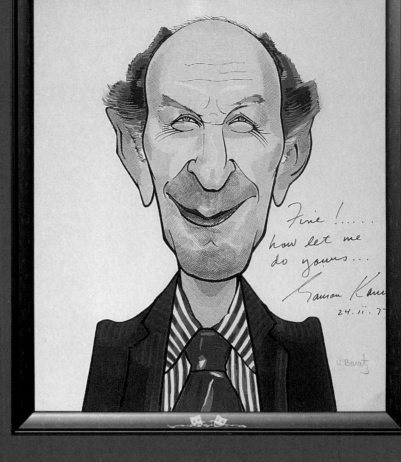

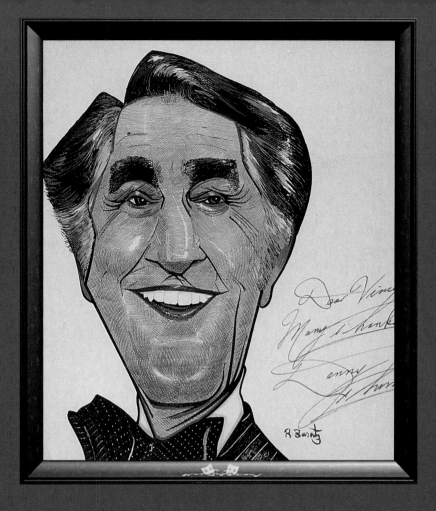

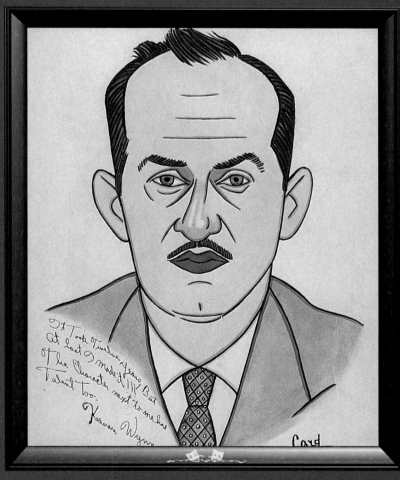

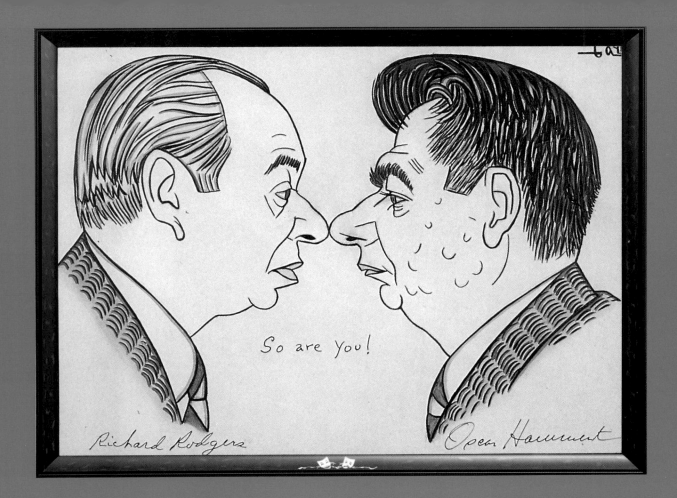

So are you!

Richard Rodgers

Oscar Hammerst [Oscar Hammerstein]

Lorenz Hart

Nowadays, come one o'clock, Sardi's and most of the midtown restaurants have turned off their lights. Back when I started out, at one o'clock people were just starting out! We used to tell people that the legal closing time was 4:00 a.m. just to get them out of here. We'd make "last call" at the bar at 3:00 a.m. Everyone who worked in the theaters in the neighborhood lived in the West Forties and Fifties then. There really was a community, a sort of club feeling about the neighborhood, too. Before Joe Allen's, there was Louis Bergen's, and next door to that was Ralph's. It's now Barrymore's. Downey's was very big over on Eighth Avenue, and there was Ryan's over there. You could go into any one of these places, and there'd be a wall-to-wall theater crowd, just like Sardi's.

There was always a crowd of Sardi's regulars who went to all the out-of-town openings. They'd phone in their responses — within half an hour of the curtain coming down in New Haven or Philly, everyone in New York knew the scoop. Back in 1943, the word on *Oklahoma!* (then called *Away We Go!*) was not good. The Shuberts wouldn't invest in the show, which was the kiss of death. Richard Rodgers and Oscar Hammerstein II played the score for Lee Shubert, and Lee fell asleep. Later, while the show was in Boston, he went around Sardi's saying, "Who wants

to see chorus girls in long dresses? Who wants a musical comedy with a funeral in the second act?" (I wonder what he would have thought about *Sweeney Todd*?) Needless to say, when it opened, it was a huge success. Lee Shubert turned to his brother and said, "Next time somebody pitches a show like that to me, I'm gonna stay awake and take it!" To which J.J. Shubert replied, "You put your money where your mouth is, and I'll put my money where your mouth is."

Dick Rodgers originally wanted his regular partner Lorenz ("Larry") Hart to write the lyrics for *Oklahoma!*. But Hart's battle with the bottle was getting the best of him. Rodgers had signed Hart up at Doctors' Hospital for a drying-out spell. In fact, they wrote most of the score for *By Jupiter* there. My mother had become Larry Hart's "second mother." When he came out of the hospital, he promised her that he had completely dried out. Yet friends would beckon him to the bar or their tables, and it wasn't long before he couldn't make it home again.

PREVIOUS PAGE: **DANNY THOMAS, MARLO THOMAS, ED WYNN, KEENAN WYNN**

THIS PAGE: **RICHARD RODGERS & OSCAR HAMMERSTEIN II, LORENZ HART**

Mother actually kept a cot made up in the restaurant's kitchen. Many a night Larry Hart slept in Sardi's.

When Dad wrote his autobiography in the 'fifties, he referred to Larry's drinking, but after the book had gone to press, he paid to have all the copies of the book recalled and reprinted without the revelations about Hart's drinking. Hart bowed out of *Oklahoma!*, and Rodgers turned to Oscar Hammerstein II, who hadn't had a big hit on Broadway since *Show Boat* in 1927. On *Oklahoma!*'s opening night, Rodgers and Hammerstein entered the lobby and headed for their table to wait for the review to come over from the *Times* building. A little man with a big cigar dashed through the crowd and embraced Dick Rodgers, gushing, "I've never had a better evening in the theater in my life! This show's gonna be around twenty years from now!" It was Larry Hart.

Oklahoma!'s sweet success also gave rise to a group at Sardi's known as the "Gloat Club." The heads of the Theater

Guild — Lawrence Langner, Armina Marshall and Terry Helburn — as well as Rodgers and Hammerstein, director Rouben Mamoulian and choreographer Agnes DeMille had a big table in the front of the restaurant. They'd all come in every day for lunch — from 1943 through 1947 — and gloat over all the other theater people who refused to invest in the show. It was at that table that Rodgers and Hammerstein brainstormed their next two shows: *Allegro* and *Carousel*.

Lawrence Langner of the Theater Guild refused to let Gard draw his caricature, or that of his wife, Armina Marshall. "You're too cruel," he told Gard. "Years from now, people who see the Sardi's caricatures will conclude that everybody in the American Theater was a thief, a hoodlum, or a cut-throat. That may be true, but I don't like to see it bandied about so openly!"

In addition to Rodgers and Hammerstein, Gard drew a few other teams such as Howard Lindsay and Russel Crouse, who wrote *Life With Father* and the book to *The Sound of Music*, among many other hits. It isn't common knowledge, but Lindsay and Crouse were also responsible for the final version of *Arsenic and Old Lace* — even though they weren't credited as such. Howard Lindsay also appeared with his wife, actress Dorothy Stickney, in *Life With Father*, but they were more celebrated for a very,

Alex Gard enlisted in the Navy. The recruiter asked him his age. Gard replied, "The Navy takes men seventeen and up. I'm up." There's a hilarious book of cartoons he drew during his stint in the Navy. When he came back from the service, he returned to his usual station at the front of Sardi's. Needless to say, there was a gap during the years he was gone.

When Gard returned, he still drew his subjects from life, as he'd always done. One of the few caricatures Alex *didn't* do in the restaurant, however, was Jimmy Walker. Mayor Walker had been a regular customer back in the early days. He was seeing actress Betty Compson, who was appearing in a show across the street. Hizzoner would have his driver park his limousine on 44th Street and would come into Sardi's and wait for her show to let out. But when Dad wanted Gard to do his caricature, the Mayor insisted that Alex go down to City Hall to sketch him. Since then, we've added a few more mayors to the walls: Robert Wagner, John Lindsay, Abe Beame, Ed Koch, and David Dinkins. We never got Fiorello LaGuardia, because he never really came into Sardi's. But we do have Tony LoBianco in full make-up *as* LaGuardia; he played "the little flower" in a one-man show on Broadway a few years ago.

without Dad urging them to "buy a bond!" Meat rationing necessitated curtailing certain dishes on the menu, and replacing them with meatless substitutes, one of which — spinach cannelloni — is still one of the most popular items on the menu.

The Sardi Bank and Trust Company's operations extended through the war. Jimmy Cannon, who was a war correspondent and later became a sports columnist for the *New York Post*, sent Dad his poker winnings, which Dad dutifully deposited in the bank. At the end of the war, Jimmy Cannon wrote Mother and Dad a letter on a sheet of Hitler's personal stationery.

After Dad closed the restaurant at night, he would spend hours sitting by himself, writing letters to the hundreds of regular customers who were stationed overseas. Although Dad read very quickly in English, writing remained a great struggle for him. Yet every night, there he'd be. One actor wrote back, saying that he found a Sardi's matchbook cover lying in the mud of a Chinese jungle!

THIS PAGE: VAN HEFLIN, ROBERT RYAN

FOLLOWING PAGE: MAYOR JIMMY WALKER, TONY LOBIANCO AS
                     FIORELLO LAGUARDIA, MAYOR JOHN V. LINDSAY,
                     MAYOR ABRAHAM BEAME

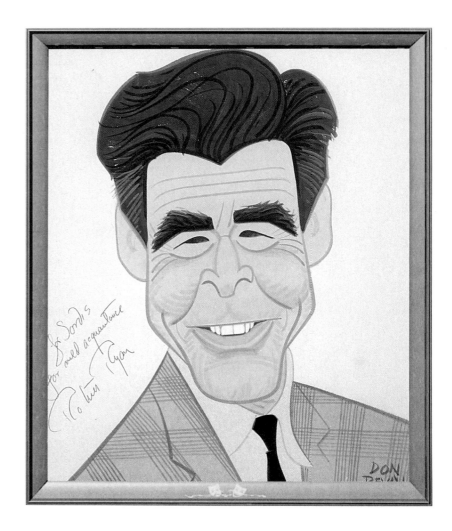

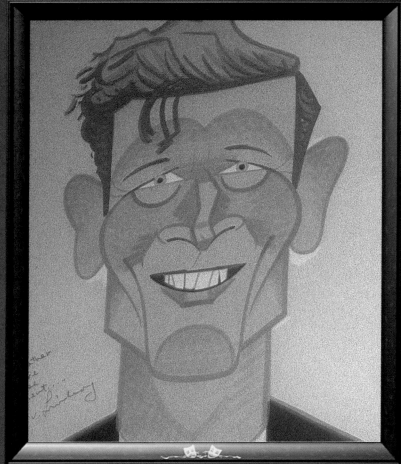

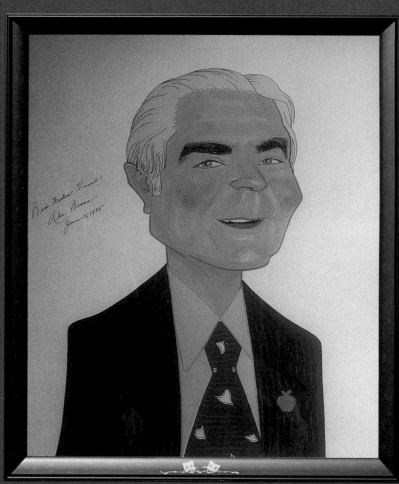

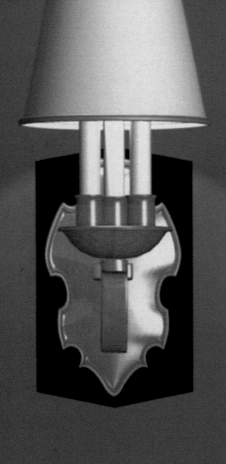

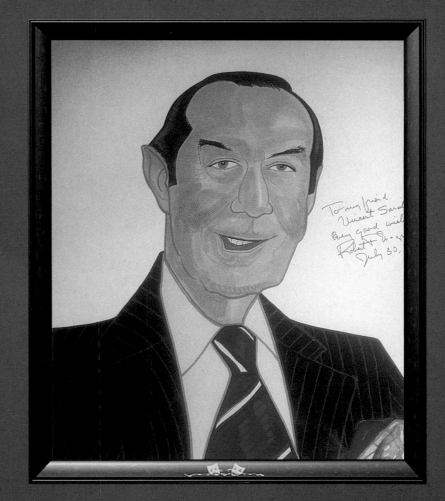

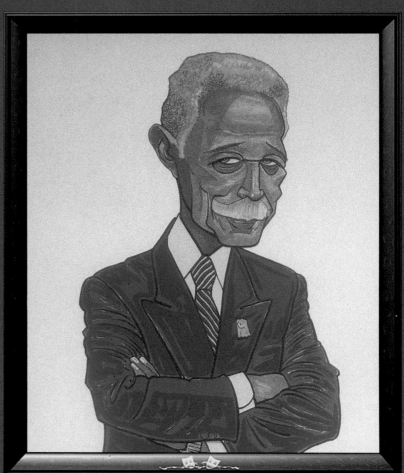

G ard was a very dapper man; he always carried a cane, and he always wore a hat. My sister Anne thought he was marvelous because of his old world manners. She would come in, on her way home from high school, put out her hand for Gard to shake, and Gard would always turn it over and kiss it. She'd practically fall through the floor. In his caricatures of women, Gard could be cruel, especially so if the woman was vain. Two cases in point: the lovely "Miss Ellie" of Dallas in her Broadway days, Barbara Bel Geddes (notice the inscription, "Oink, oink!") and Gard's friend and fellow Russian, the great ballerina Tamara Geva ("Blame my parents"). It was odd that such a dapper fellow should claim such a distaste for vanity of any kind. But that was Alex Gard.

Of course, actors have to be vain. They're in the vanity business. Gard delighted in touching their most sensitive points. He didn't stop with actors, though; producer Sam Harris was a very distinguished theater man, but he was also a notorious slob. So Gard drew him with spaghetti hanging out of his mouth, unshaven, really gross. But Sam liked it, and signed it.

For the longest time, Gard had kept two spaces reserved near the front for Mother and Dad, but he never seemed to get around to doing them. So many of his subjects were upset by their caricatures; maybe he thought Mother and Dad would be, too. Finally, when Dad and Mother threatened to put Lee Shubert in the spot of honor, Gard drew them immediately. Today they're right near the coat check. You can't miss them as you come in. I think despite Gard's unsentimental style, he was a bit of a marshmallow when it came to my parents.

W hen I took over the restaurant after the Second World War, I wanted to change the terms of Gard's contract. I told him, "Alex, things are different now; we're busy, we're making money; there's no reason to have this barter deal. Why don't you just set a price per caricature and we'll pay you?" Alex replied, "A contract is a contract," and kept to his agreement with Dad till the day he died.

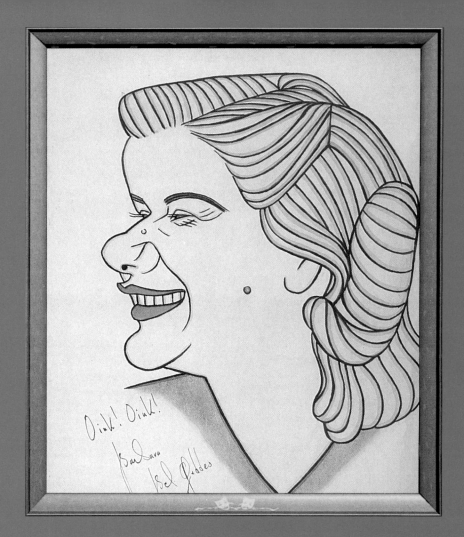

PREVIOUS PAGE: MAYOR ROBERT WAGNER, MAYOR
EDWARD I. KOCH, MAYOR DAVID DINKINS

THIS PAGE: BARBARA BEL GEDDES, ALFRED DRAKE

Alex collapsed in the Times Square subway station in 1948. He died in the ambulance on the way to the hospital. He had no family. No one was really that close to him. My sister Anne remembers a woman who had something to do with the New York City Ballet School; she remembers thinking of this woman as "Mrs. Gard." But there never was a "Mrs. Gard." When Anne would ask Alex about this woman — after they'd split — he'd just say "Nyet" and refuse to talk.

Alex left five caricatures unfinished when he died. We hung them on the walls in their incomplete state. Wendy Hiller was his last caricature, but Alfred Drake and Jessica Tandy were also left undone. If you'll look at the pencil sketches, you'll see that they're signed in ink. Alex worked in the restaurant, drawing the subjects from life. When he'd finished the pencil drawing, he would prevail upon the subject to sign it. Only then would he take it away and finish it. He wrote instructions for himself — in Russian, of, course — and then inked the final version at home. After laying in the color, he'd dunk the drawing in the bathtub, and then dry it out. If the colors ran or faded, he applied them again, repeating the whole process until he had the caricature just the way he wanted it. He used to say, "The Sardi's caricatures will retain their color even if they were kept at the bottom of the ocean for twenty years." I suppose if New York is ever hit by a tidal wave, the Gards will survive.

By the way, since Gard left Jessica Tandy's caricature unfinished, I had John Mackey do her again, this time in color, but I didn't like it much, and neither did she. Nonetheless, we put it up along with Gard's. Then I asked Hume Cronyn if I could do his caricature, and he turned me down. "You've already got two pictures of my wife," he explained, "so why do you need one of me?"

Alex Gard drew the first seven hundred and twenty caricatures in our collection during his twenty-one years at Sardi's. When he died, the era of the caricatures was over — only Gard could make a Sardi's caricature, or so it seemed at the time. The very idea of replacing Alex Gard was sacrilegious.

THIS PAGE: JESSICA TANDY, DAME WENDY HILLER

FOLLOWING PAGE: SIR ALEC GUINNESS, ROBERT MORLEY,
                     DAME EDITH EVANS

67

I'm not even surprised!
Alec Guin...

Mackey

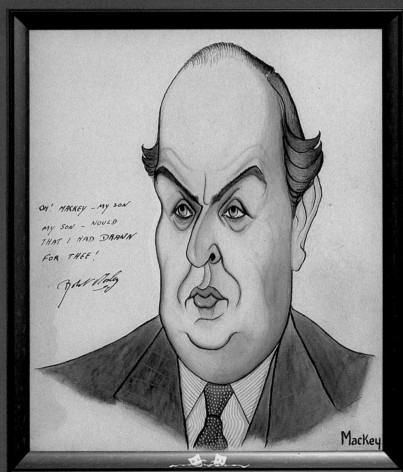

OH! MACKEY — MY SON
MY SON — WOULD
THAT I HAD DRAWN
FOR THEE!

Mackey

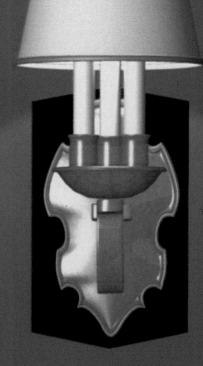

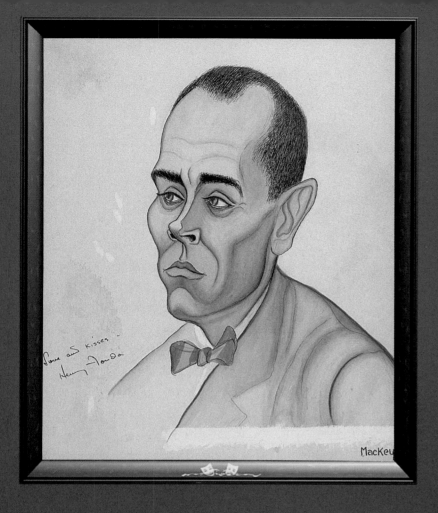

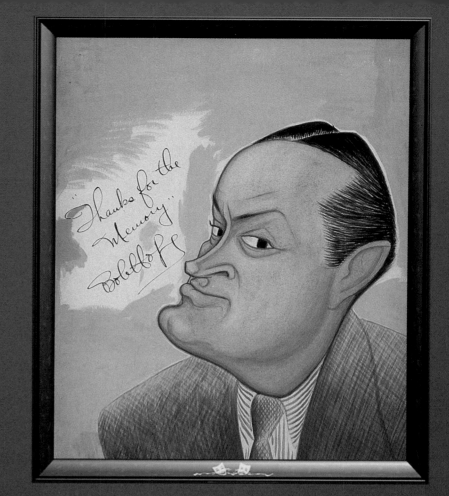

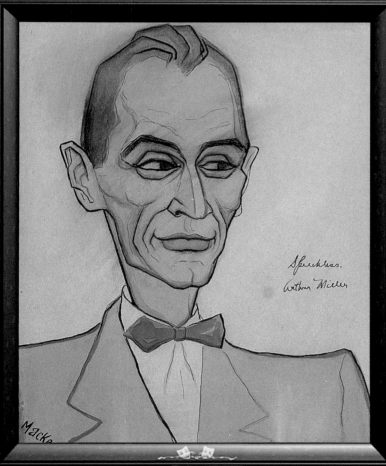

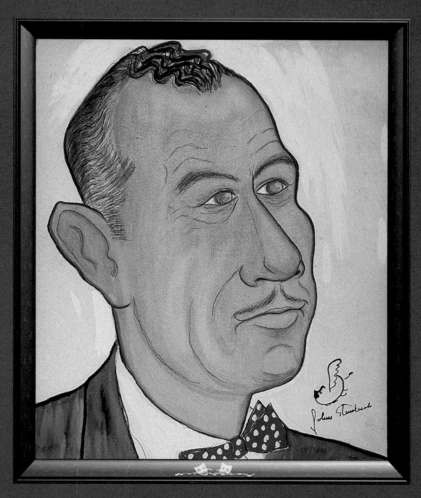

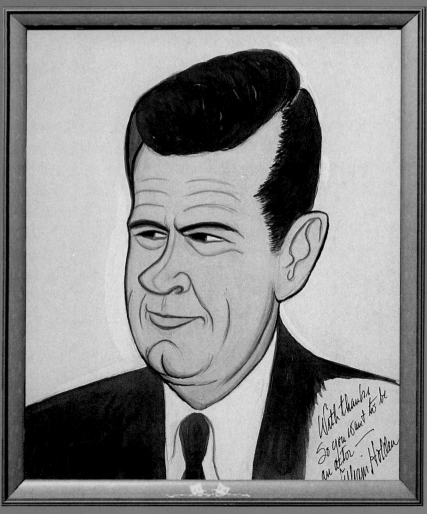

After a year or two, I started to feel a lot of pressure from the regulars to revive the tradition. And it was suddenly clear that our walls — which had for years reflected all the changes of scenery in New York — had stopped capturing those changes.

After the war, musicals started to become the mainstay of Broadway, and there was a whole new brand of straight play coming up — this was the time of Tennessee Williams and Arthur Miller. A lot of bright new actors were being seen in the fledgling Off-Broadway movement — and there was this novelty called television that was gaining in popularity.

I asked Al Hirschfeld to take over, but Al worked on a scale that looked right for the *Times*, and his style was really suited to black-and-white. Al Capp really wanted the job, too, but the demands of his comic strip *Li'l Abner* prevented him from taking it. I found a chap named John Mackey to take Gard's place. He did some major figures of the time: Henry Fonda, Ethel Merman, Bob Hope, Alec Guinness, Josh Logan and John Steinbeck. I guess I might have been disappointed with any artist after Alex, but it wasn't long before I bade Mr. Mackey farewell. What's more, Mackey liked to drink a bit too much; I suppose I'm like Dad when it comes to drinking in the restaurant. It's one thing for the patrons, but another when it's the caricaturist, representing Sardi's.

One big star of the time Mackey did was William Holden. For all his leading-man looks, Bill Holden had a dark, brooding, wild side. More than once during a location shoot, he had to be pulled in from a window sill or hotel balcony, where he was hanging, Harold Lloyd-style. Yet most of the time he was well-mannered and truly, painfully shy. During a visit to New York he was invited to Sardi's to a party thrown in honor of Pearl Bailey. He entered the restaurant and pasted himself to the walls of the lobby, afraid to go up to the second-floor party. Finally, he spotted an old friend, the wife of a film studio publicist. He nearly dragged her upstairs, explaining, "I want you to walk in with me."

PREVIOUS PAGE: **HENRY FONDA, BOB HOPE, ARTHUR MILLER, JOHN STEINBECK**

THIS PAGE: **ETHEL MERMAN, WILLIAM HOLDEN**

Most people think of actors as extroverts, show-offs; but I think a lot of the great actors go on stage to overcome their basic shyness. Often when big stars come into Sardi's they look extremely shy and lost. It helps if one of our waiters recognizes them and speaks to them by name. Actors and actresses are easier to please than the average businessman. They have to deal with so much rejection and coldness in their business, they are more appreciative of even the smallest kindness. So many of our best performers spend a lot of time "at liberty." I've learned to be awfully careful with an actor out of work. A table in a good location is simply my way of giving him a pat on the back.

By the way, in his movie debut, the film of Clifford Odets' *Golden Boy* in 1937, William Holden's father was played by Group Theater (and Sardi's) regular Lee J. Cobb. What's unusual about that? Holden was twenty-one, and Cobb was all of twenty-eight! I can top that. Broadway's beloved Angela Lansbury was only three years older than Laurence Harvey when she played his mother in the film of Dick Condon's *Manchurian Candidate*.

On our radio show, *Luncheon at Sardi's*, Nancy Olson recalled a practical joke on the set of *Sunset Boulevard* in 1950. Miss Olson, who was married to Alan Jay Lerner at the time, co-starred with William Holden. The film's director, Billy Wilder, insisted on a closed set while shooting, but Lerner managed to crash the doors of the soundstage and keep an eye on his young bride.

Wilder was aware of Lerner's presence on the set, but never acknowledged him until the day came to shoot a love scene between the two young stars. Wilder directed Holden to kiss Mrs. Lerner, and the kiss kept going long after the camera stopped turning — a minute, then two, three, four. Lerner grew livid with jealousy until Holden let him know that it was all for his benefit. Then Wilder let Holden know that he had invited Brenda Marshall (Mrs. Holden) to watch that day's filming!

THIS PAGE: **AL HIRSCHFELD, PADDY CHAYEVSKY**

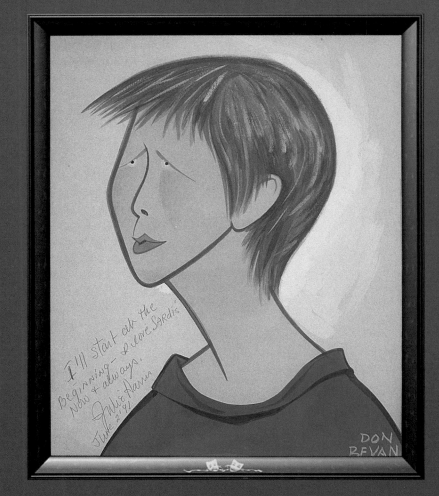

I suppose everybody knows about the opening night parties at Sardi's. After all, the *Times* is just next door, and all the papers get rushed here just as soon as they're printed. Well, when Henry Fonda's daughter Jane made her Broadway debut, Hank tried to talk her out of coming to the restaurant after the show. He knew what would happen when the papers came out. Sure enough, the party was going loud and strong till the press agent's head gofer brought in the dailies. Everyone took a look at the reviews, and Jane burst into tears. Not another word was said. Everybody left. Party over. It happens; and not just in the movies, either.

It's funny about opening nights. There are two distinct tempos after an opening. First, the audience arrives in Sardi's after the curtain with a buzz of excitement, which reaches a climax as the featured players, then the stars, enter, each one getting an ovation. It's funny, but sometimes the one who gets the biggest ovation doesn't have his or her name above the title. Often it's someone in a small role who scores the biggest hit with the audience.

The second round of excitement comes later, when the first papers arrive, or — as is more likely today — the evening news programs come on with their reviews. But it's still the *Times* that counts. Back in the old days, when there were a lot more papers, the first copies off the presses were rushed right to Sardi's. No doubt rumors about the reviews will have circulated, since the critics may have seen the show during its last few previews, but it ain't over till the *Times* sings.

You can always tell how the box office is going to behave the next day by what happens in Sardi's after the reviews come out. If they're good, we start to hear, "Captain, a bottle of champagne and the food menu. God, I'm hungry!" If the reviews aren't good, all we hear is "Check, please."

FACING PAGE: CLAIRE BLOOM, JULIE HARRIS, LEE REMICK, SHELLEY WINTERS

THIS PAGE: AN OPENING NIGHT PARTY: NEIL SIMON TALKS WITH VINCENT SARDI, JR., MIKE NICHOLS IS AT RIGHT

FOLLOWING PAGE: RICARDO MONTALBAN, ALAN ALDA, BLYTHE DANNER, DIANA SANDS

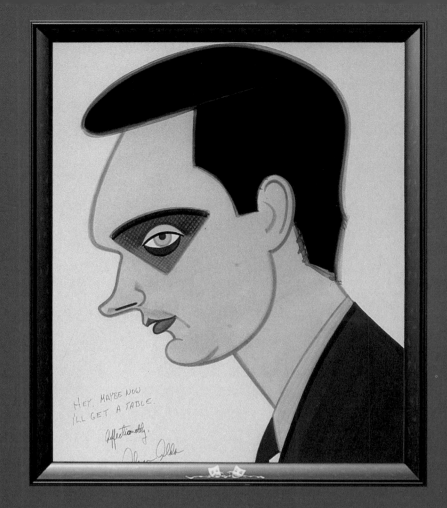

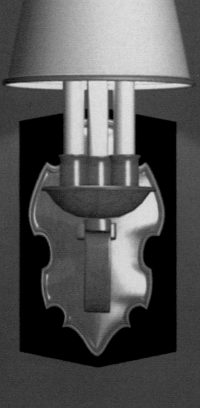

Anne Bancroft

DON BEVAN

DON BEVAN

Vincent, I'm proud to be
hangin' on your wall!
Lloyd Bridges

The tradition of stars receiving standing ovations in Sardi's after an opening night performance started in 1950 with Shirley Booth. Shirley, whom you'll probably best remember as "Hazel" in the TV sit-com of the same name in the 1960's, was a faithful customer from the earliest days when she was a regular on Ed Gardner's *Duffy's Tavern* radio show. (Shirley was married to Ed Gardner at the time.) In 1950, she had just triumphed in William Inge's *Come Back Little Sheba*, and after the show she came into the restaurant with her agent, William Liebling, and Liebling's wife (and Inge's agent), Audrey Wood.

I wasn't expecting Shirley and hadn't saved a good front table for her. She didn't care where she sat — so I sent her to a table in the back corner, where she usually liked to sit anyway. As she made her way across the floor, everyone who had seen her performance stood and applauded. Well, Shirley kept turning around and looking toward the door to see whom they were applauding.

She figured that someone like Eleanor Roosevelt had come in. Liebling pointed out to Shirley that everyone was applauding her, but Shirley just couldn't believe it. She never lost her genuine humility, even after she'd won the Tony and, later, the Oscar for her touching performance in *Little Sheba*.

Over the years I've had squabbles with press agents and managers who insist that their star clients get front tables after a show. I maintain that if they want their clients to get a big reception, the stars should cross the room to a back table, but the agents insist on the front. You can guess what happens. The stars are ushered to the front, and nobody else in the restaurant knows they're there. Then the agents wonder why nobody notices them!

After Mackey, I needed to find yet another caricaturist. Jack Kirkland, who wrote the long-running stage version of *Tobacco Road*, recommended his new son-in-law, who had just lost his job with a minor movie studio, Eagle Lion Films. I knew Kirkland, and I knew his daughter, Patricia, who was making a name for herself as a Broadway actress. I didn't know Jack's son-in-law, a talented commercial artist named Donald Bevan — but Don Bevan knew Sardi's.

PREVIOUS PAGE: ANNE BANCROFT, JAMES EARL JONES, LLOYD BRIDGES

THIS PAGE: SHIRLEY BOOTH, DONALD BEVAN

Don was not in the war as an artist; he served as a gunner in General "Twelve O'clock High" Armstrong's right wing. While flying a mission over Germany in 1943, he was shot down, captured by the Nazis, and put into a prisoner of war camp with some British prisoners. Later, he was moved to another camp in Krems, Austria, which the Germans referred to as "Stalag XVII." Sound familiar?

Don entertained his fellow detainees with his witty caricatures of their group. Later, after he was freed, he sent the drawings back to the families of his fellow prisoners as a special memento. Unfortunately, the mothers of some of the boys thought that Don's distortions reflected their sons' actual conditions!

To combat the fatigue of imprisonment, Bevan and fellow prisoner Edmund Trzcinski decided to pool their talents and build a theater. Don put his art-school training together with his love of the theater and the experience gained in his stint one summer as a stage manager in Mount Holyoke, and assembled a stage from International Red Cross crates. He managed to make *papier-mâché* sets and props from waste paper. An Australian designer in the camp made costumes out of bandage gauze dyed with yellow and purple salve. Samuel French

When Don came to New York, he first got to know the restaurant by following his favorite stars to our front door after a matinee. The stars crossed the threshold. Bevan still considered himself an outsider. One world war later, however, Don's theatrical and artistic career would bring him into Sardi's in his own right.

If he hadn't become our caricaturist, who knows, Don might have become a matinee idol. You can see from his photo that he was a great looking guy. There was never any question that he belonged in the theater in *some* capacity. From the moment he stumbled into a job as a stage manager in summer stock in 1939, Bevan's course in the theater was marked.

When he first entered the service, Bevan did portraits of enlisted men for the combat room. A war correspondent named Walter Cronkite was impressed by their unusual quality, and began to feed them to his wire service. It was through Cronkite that Bevan's work was first published.

THIS PAGE: WALTER CRONKITE, MIKE WALLACE
FOLLOWING PAGE: EARTHA KITT, ROBERT MORSE, BEN VEREEN

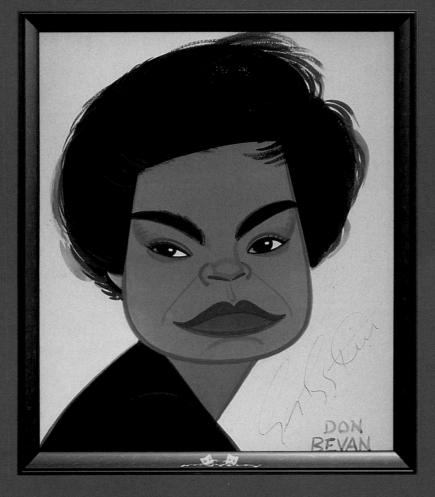

DON
BEVAN

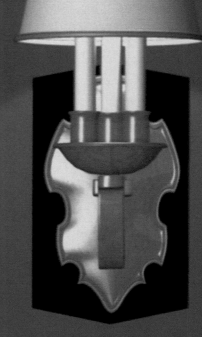

DON
BEVAN

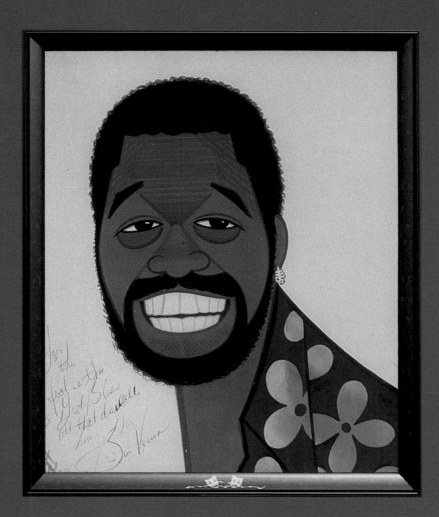

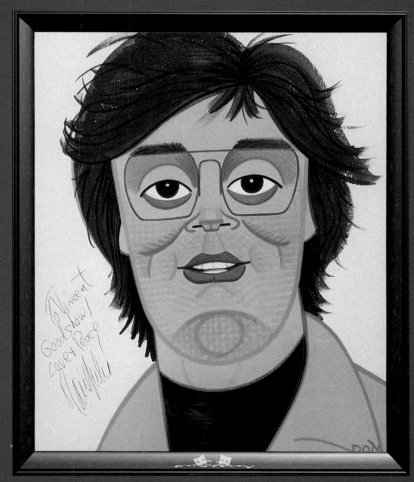

playscripts penetrated enemy lines courtesy of the Red Cross.

In their two years in the camp, the boys produced ten shows — a better record than many New York producers at the time!. They put on full-length plays, as well as revues with sketches written by Ed and Don — each of which played about twelve performances to a maximum of 400 fellow prisoners.

All the women's roles were, naturally, played by young men in drag, Elizabethan-style. The Nazis required the cross-dressed actors to hand over their costumes immediately after each performance — to prevent G.I.s from escaping disguised as women.

One night Don and Ed, absorbed in the aftermath of a particularly lively performance, stayed out beyond their barracks curfew. To return past curfew would have risked being shot by the Nazi guards. The two young impresarios wound up staying all night in their makeshift playhouse. They began to brainstorm about their own dramatic circumstances. They'd been so preoccupied with creating conventional sketches about life outside the camp, they hadn't appreciated that their own lives inside the camp were made of vibrant theatrical stuff. By the next morning they had a rough sketch of the comic melodrama that would become the hit Broadway play, Stalag 17.

Don and Ed wrote the first draft of their play, carefully censoring any references too damaging to the Nazis, in case their captors confiscated and read the first draft. (They did.) Then, on May 3, 1945, General Patton and his men liberated Stalag 17. Don and Ed were free men. After arriving in Paris, they wasted no time in writing a second draft, restoring everything they couldn't let the Nazis read. They were aided in their efforts by another American stationed in Paris — Col. Joshua Logan — the gifted director and co-author of South Pacific. Logan read their drafts and urged the budding playwrights to mix raucous barracks humor with the intense drama of the prison camp.

That reminds me of a story about Josh Logan. He was in Sardi's one night when a drunken patron wobbled up to him

PREVIOUS PAGE: DIAHANN CARROLL, RICHARD KILEY, JOEL GREY, RAUL JULIA

THIS PAGE: JOSHUA LOGAN, GEORGE ABBOTT

and slurred, "Josh, old pal, you're the best director alive, the very, very best. I can't think of anyone better." "What about Elia Kazan?" Josh asked. The drunk took a long pause. "Josh, old pal," he said, "you're right."

When Don came back to the States, he started working for *The Daily News* as a result of the caricatures that Cronkite had sent back home. Before long, the *Baltimore Sun* came sniffing around Don to find out if he'd be willing to become their new editorial cartoonist. As a first assignment, the paper sent Don to the 1948 presidential conventions in Philadelphia, where he holed up in a hotel suite with, of all people, Alistair Cooke and H.L. Mencken.

Don decided that he really didn't want to move to Baltimore, and, after working out of New York for a while, realized that he couldn't really stand the pace. So he went to work for Eagle Lion creating poster art and lobby cards. Every night, after he finished his ad work, he would rush across town to work with Ed Trzcinski on *Stalag 17*. Ed's family owned a funeral parlor, and the two authors would work upstairs at night. Once they had polished several pages, they would invite actor friends over and read the play aloud, a piece at a time.

An amateur theater group in Philadelphia called "Plays and Players" was the first to produce the play. This group wasn't really the right bunch for *Stalag 17*, since they were mostly Main Liners who produced Restoration Comedy in a tiny, elegant playhouse that once belonged to the Shuberts.

Ed and Don went down to see a rehearsal and were appalled. The director had excised most of the strong language and low comedy of the play so as not to offend the troupe's genteel subscribers, and had a rather refined brain surgeon playing the cynical, hard-bitten leading character. Don and Ed got some of the actors replaced, injected a little G.I. feeling into the remaining cast, and "enhanced" the director's misguided efforts with a helping hand from their pal Frank Corsaro.

THIS PAGE: JED HARRIS, ALEXANDER COHEN
FOLLOWING PAGE: PHIL SILVERS, SID CAESAR, IMOGENE COCA

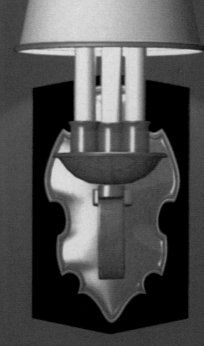

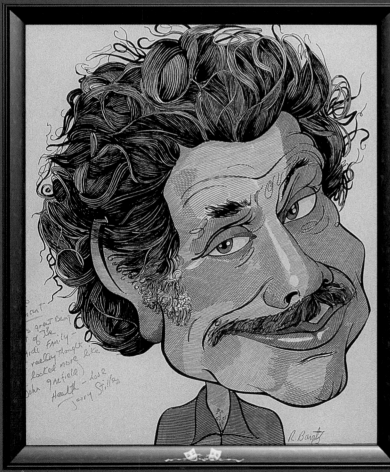

*Okay, Bevan—
you'll write a play
someday—
Walter Kerr*

DON
BEVAN

During all this, Don was working for me at Sardi's, turning out roughly a caricature a month. I now chose Don's subjects; he only blanched when I asked him to caricature a critic. No doubt Bevan the playwright was afraid that Bevan the caricaturist would offend one of the critics, who would exact his revenge in a review of Don's play.

Don's wife Patricia became a network casting director, so both of the Bevans kept close tabs on promising young talent by seeing all of the new shows on and off Broadway. I know Gard did a caricature of Mrs. Bevan during her acting days, but it rather mysteriously disappeared when Don retired.

By the way, for a number of years I bought tickets to all the new shows for the restaurant staff, so that they'd recognize the actors and actresses as they came in. But now, it seems, the staff knows most of the celebrities from movies and TV.

PREVIOUS PAGE: MARY TYLER MOORE, DICK VAN DYKE,
                   JERRY STILLER, ANNE MEARA

THIS PAGE: WALTER KERR, KERR AND RICHARD WATTS, JR.
                   IN THE SECOND FLOOR BAR

FACING PAGE: ANTHONY PERKINS, RAYMOND BURR,
                   HAL HOLBROOK

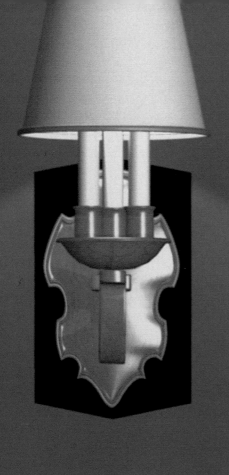

Returning to New York, Don and Ed offered their play to several producers and directors. They succeeded in getting the play optioned repeatedly by several managements, but none of them bit the bullet when it came to raising money. Everyone thought the play was good, but, alas, had no commercial appeal.

Don and Ed finally engaged former *wunderkind* Jed Harris to direct a production featuring the junior members of the Lambs Club in the club's own theater. Although Harris was a brilliant and innovative director (he produced and directed, among others, *The Front Page* and Thornton Wilder's *Our Town*), he was despised by many actors, even to the extent that Laurence Olivier, when playing Richard the Third, simply made himself up to look like Jed Harris. It's also rumored that the Disney animators used Harris as their model for the Big Bad Wolf.

Jed Harris saw the prisoners of *Stalag* 17 as caged animals, pacing slowly in their cages, and spent the first two weeks of a three-week rehearsal period staging the first scene of the play. He then simply got tired of his own routine and stopped showing up at rehearsals. Simply vanished. Don and Ed managed to pull the show together and brought José Ferrer to see it. Ferrer pounced on the play, and decided to direct and co-produce it

on Broadway. The play opened six years and five days after the real Stalag XVII was liberated by Patton. It ran on Broadway for 59 weeks (472 performances), then toured.

Despite its success in the U.S., it played only nine performances in London. I suppose the war-weary British didn't want to see such a grim — if lively — reminder of their own suffering during the war. In 1952, an amateur Army Special Services company toured the play through Korea. And, of course, *Stalag* 17 became a Billy Wilder film which won William Holden the Academy Award for best actor.

The first caricature Don did for the walls of Sardi's was of Denholm Elliott, the delightful British character actor, who was a guest at his father-in-law's house. The second was of Maureen Stapleton, and you know what happened to that one. Don remembers Maureen's as too small in the frame, and says it was before he really developed a style, but I remember it as a good one.

In fact, Don says that he had to force a style onto himself at the beginning. He figured that it was important to find out what each person was like, for the success of a caricature depends

THIS PAGE: **JIMMY MOLINSKY WITH YUL BRYNNER, HELEN HAYES**

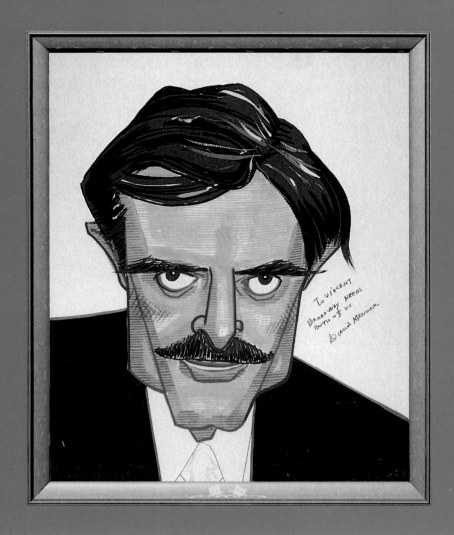

he was the greatest judge of art, which suited Don. Don would bring Jimmy a caricature, and hold it up across the room, and ask him, "Who is this?" If Jimmy knew who it was instantly, Don figured that he'd captured his subject. If Jimmy didn't recognize who it was, Don figured it was "too artistic" and started over.

Don's touch was a good deal gentler and more whimsical than Gard's. Helen Hayes was coming down the stairs from the second floor with some friends one evening, and didn't know Don was in the restaurant. Helen and her friends stopped to look at the new caricatures on display at the front of the restaurant. Don overheard Helen say, "Oh, I wish that darling Don Bevan had done mine. He has such a sense of humor!" As you can see from Gard's caricature of Helen, it's devastating.

David Merrick was always a good customer. He actually campaigned to have his caricature done. I finally had Don draw him, but then Merrick wouldn't sign it. My deal with Don was that no caricature went on the wall until it was signed, so Don did another, more flattering version of Merrick, then another. No go. Don finally gave up. We eventually hung Merrick up unsigned, until it moved to the Alberghetti gallery. Lately I had our current caricaturist, Richard Baratz, do Merrick again, and this time he signed.

on how much of the personality the artist can capture. Don would go to each actor's press agent and get photographs, but photographs — especially of actors and actresses — can conceal the truth. A lot of press agents let Don go through their files until he found what he wanted.

Don would go to a matinee to watch the performer in action, with the caricature in mind. He'd sit there with his binoculars, sketching, then he'd meet the actor in his dressing room after the show. Don told his subject that he was there to sketch, but he was really there to get to know the person behind the performance. He would then start with very small drawings, keeping it simple, so that he could get the essence of the actor or actress on paper; then he'd blow that drawing up to the full size. He always kept in mind that the caricatures had to "read" from the other side of a crowded dining room.

When Don was finished, he'd use Jimmy Molinsky, our *maitre d'*, as his acid test. Jimmy started at Sardi's as a bartender's assistant in 1938, and stayed with us until he retired in 1980. Jimmy knew all the regular patrons, but I wouldn't say that

THIS PAGE: DAVID MERRICK, JOSEPH PAPP

FOLLOWING PAGE: NEIL SIMON, INGRID BERGMAN

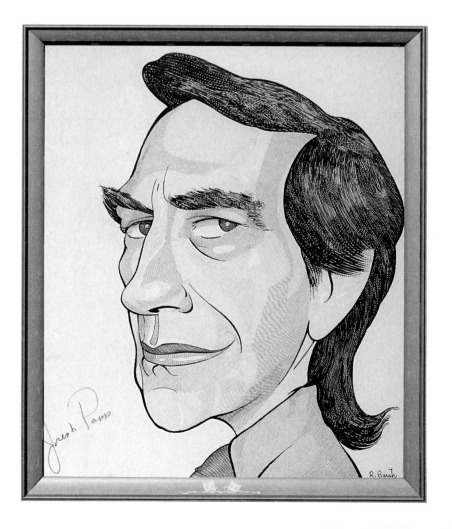

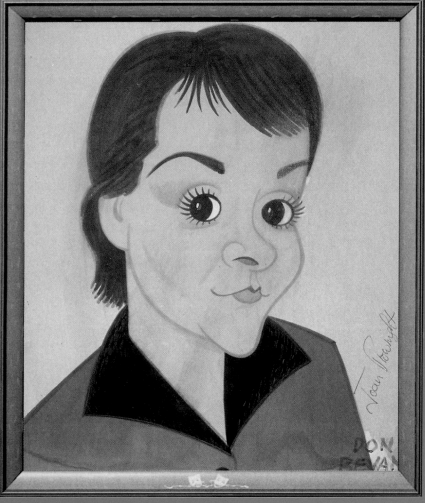

More recently, David Merrick had a significant hand in the history of Sardi's. A few years ago I sold the restaurant to a group of investors; things didn't work out well, and I had to go to court to regain the restaurant, during which time our doors were closed. We were about to re-open when David wanted to hold the opening-night party for his Broadway revival of *Oh, Kay!* at Sardi's. Thanks to that master showman's savvy, we re-opened Sardi's with a gala cast party on November 1, 1990. For a while thereafter, we didn't have a liquor license, so many of the regular patrons of "The Little Bar" brought their own hand-labeled bottles and stowed them behind the bar — for private consumption only.

I'd known Leonard Bernstein since he was a student of Koussevitsky's at Tanglewood. Lenny wanted to be done, enough to call Don Bevan himself to set up the appointment. Don went to Lenny's house, where the maestro was watching the World Series. He asked Don how long it would take, and Don said "about a half hour." Well, don't you know, exactly a half hour later, after a lot of friendly chat and small talk, Lenny said, "Time's up," and that was that. Don finished the caricature; either Lenny didn't like it, or his sister didn't like it; but Lenny never signed it. He forbade me to put it up on the walls. Well, Don liked it, and I liked it, so it went up anyway.

Years later, shortly before Bernstein died, he came into the restaurant. He'd been to see a play with his sister, and he was coming out of the restaurant, looking for his limo. My wife June and I were standing there as well, and he came up to me and threw his arms around me. As you can surmise from his music, Bernstein was a very emotional fellow. We chatted, and talked over old times, and he was as warm and effusive as ever. The next day, he came back. In my absence, he went up to George, the night manager, and said, "Tell Vincent that I've come here for fifty years, and he's still never done a caricature of me!" I called him the next day and told him, "Lenny, not only have we had your caricature up for years, you've never signed it!" He said he would, but he never got around to it. At least he knew it was there.

PREVIOUS PAGE: LEONARD BERNSTEIN, LAURENCE OLIVIER
THIS PAGE: ANTHONY QUINN, JOAN PLOWRIGHT

Don also did Richard Burton, who was a genuinely lovely man. He was known around town as a great tipper, and all of the theater doormen wanted to get Burton into their houses, because he was so generous and grateful to them. Doormen at the Broadway theaters often perform a lot of personal tasks for stars, sometimes without even a word of thanks, but not so with Burton.

Don went to Burton's apartment to sketch, and Burton asked him, "Have you done Larry yet?" referring to Laurence Olivier, who was on Broadway in Jean Anouilh's *Becket*. "No," Don replied, "he isn't a customer of Sardi's, and that's what it's all about."

Burton must have said something to "Larry" about his caricature, because Olivier called Don Bevan up and invited him to lunch. Not at Sardi's, mind you, but at the Horn & Hardart automat! As it turned out, Olivier liked eating there not only because of a deep-seated British tightness, but because among the taxi drivers, no one would know who he was. I'm sure Olivier could relax in the Automat in a way he couldn't anywhere else.

Sir Laurence (he became a Lord much later) was incensed that we had done a caricature of his co-star in *Becket*, Anthony Quinn, who *was* a regular, but we'd never done him. We had Gielgud, Redgrave, Alec Guinness, but no Olivier. Although Don still doesn't think he really captured his subject, the great actor himself was delighted. When he came in to sign the caricature, Olivier dated it 1929 — the year in which he made his Broadway debut — in order to correct a long-neglected oversight.

A friend of Don Bevan's once spotted Olivier shopping down on the Lower East Side, being trailed by this tiny lady from the neighborhood. She was right on Olivier's heels, trying to get a peek at his face. Olivier tried to avoid her, but he made a wrong turn and she ended up face to face with her idol, and all she could do was moan, "Oy, oy, oy, it's him! Oy, oy, oy!"

THIS PAGE: ALBERT FINNEY, JOHN HOUSEMAN
FOLLOWING PAGE: CHITA RIVERA, GWEN VERDON

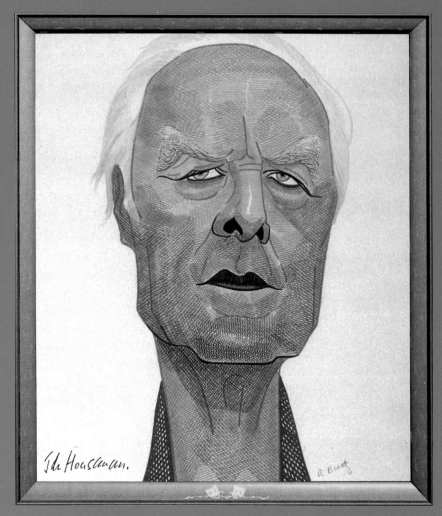

The surprising thing about stars — who live in the limelight most of the time — is that they really value their privacy. After Don Bevan had done Richard Burton's caricature, Don and his wife were dining at Sardi's, and Burton was seated several tables away. Burton saw Don and came over to thank him for his caricature, and Don temporarily blanked on Burton's name. Couldn't remember it to save his life. Don was mortified, but Burton cheerfully introduced himself, chuckling. Burton was happy to be anonymous, if only for a second.

I suppose I realized that the restaurant had become known around the world when I received a letter from a woman in Japan, addressed to "Mr. Vincent Saldy, Owner, Famous Restaurant, Broadway, USA."

Don Bevan had an unexpected surprise when he did John Lindsay's caricature. Don was impressed by the dashing mayor's leading-man looks, and made him look like a matinee idol. When Don finished the drawing, he showed it to Lindsay and his wife, who weren't amused. "Try it again, and this time be more ruthless. I'm a politician, for God's sake, not an actor!"

Don was in the restaurant when President and Mrs. Truman were having a quiet dinner. Don tried not to gawk, but he couldn't help noticing that the Trumans were looking up at the caricatures. Mr. Truman pointed toward Gard's caricature of Mayor Jimmy Walker — who was a notorious ladies' man — and whispered something into Mrs. Truman's ear. Don couldn't hear what Mr. Truman said, but Bess gave the President a playful, "stop it" kind of slap on the cheek.

Pearl Bailey signed her caricature, but she ran down the whole litany of defective features: "Gosh, it isn't my mouth, it isn't my nose, those aren't my eyes" and so on. Neil Simon's press agent couldn't understand why "Doc" liked his caricature, but he did, and Don did, too. Ingrid Bergman was very happy

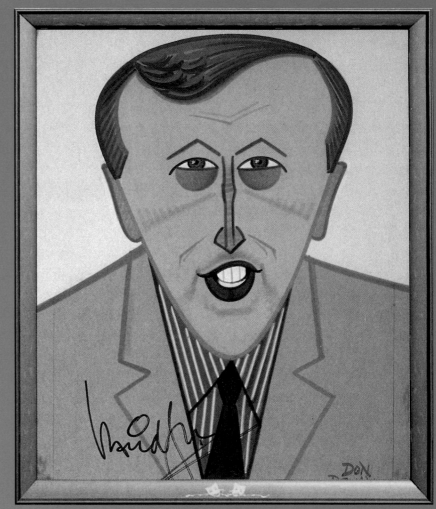

PREVIOUS PAGE: ANN MILLER, PEARL BAILEY

THIS PAGE: JACK PAAR, DAVID FROST

with hers, spent a lot of time sitting for Don, and was very appreciative when she signed. But when Don brought it to the restaurant and we put it up, one of the bartenders was mad as hell at Don for what he'd done to Miss Bergman.

Don was sitting in Sardi's with a friend one day between the luncheon and dinner shifts, when Marilyn Monroe came in for dinner with her press agent. Monroe was dressed very sedately in an elegant tan suit, and obviously wanted to be inconspicuous. Don's friend, who had met Monroe in Hollywood, went over to say hello. Monroe was very gracious, and then Don and his friend left and went to "21," where John Huston was having a party to celebrate the premiere of his film of *Moby Dick*. The party was well under way when Monroe came in. She didn't recognize anyone in the room but Don and his friend, so she went over to them and asked, "Who's the party for?" Don's friend answered, "It's a party for *Moby Dick*." "Who's that?" asked Monroe. Don said, "He's a whale — a big, white whale." "You're kidding!" gasped Monroe. "I came to a party for a goddamn *fish*?"

Somewhere around that same time, I took my family out to the West Coast for a holiday, and we were given a tour of the Paramount lot. Well, at the time, I was *au courant* with the opera and the theater, but I hadn't been to the movies much. The guide kept showing us movie sets, telling us which films they were for, but I hadn't seen a one of them. After four or five such incidents, our flustered guide was ready to give up. In desperation, he took us to a soundstage where a film was actually shooting. After a long day of frustration, our guide was astonished when most of the actors swarmed around me. "Vincent! Good to see you!" "How's New York?" "Can't wait to get back to God's country!"

Perhaps it was at that moment that I decided to include current movie and TV people in our gallery.

THIS PAGE: **MERV GRIFFIN, DICK CAVETT**

95

Today in "The Little Bar" we have four caricatures hanging up over the bar itself. You'll certainly recognize them as *The Honeymooners*: Jackie Gleason, Audrey Meadows, Art Carney and Joyce Randolph. Still, we didn't do them as a group during the run of the TV series.

Gleason was done when he was starring on Broadway in *Take Me Along*, which explains why he's sporting a mustache. The rest of the cast have all worked on Broadway as well. In fact, everybody can identify Jack Lemmon and Walter Matthau from the movie *The Odd Couple*, and Tony Randall and Jack Klugman as their TV counterparts, but most people don't realize that, on Broadway, Walter Matthau and Art Carney were the original *Odd Couple*.

Speaking of little-known facts, we also have a *fifth* Honeymooner's caricature up on the second floor. Before Audrey Meadows, the first Alice Kramden was a delightful character actress named Pert Kelton, whom you might remember from the Broadway and Hollywood versions of *The Music Man* (she played Mrs. Paroo).

A rumor circulated that Gleason dropped Pert from the original show because she was on a McCarthy blacklist, but it was actually because of a heart condition that made it difficult for Pert to keep up a live TV schedule. She turned up on *The Honeymooners* again some years later — playing Alice Kramden's mother. While we're on the subject, we also have the *first* Trixie Norton on the walls — in one early episode only, she was played by Elaine Stritch.

Jackie Gleason never did anything in a small way; when he came in to sign his caricature, he threw quite a party. During the years when his TV show originated in New York, when the pressure got to be too much for "The Great One," Gleason would check himself into a suite of rooms at a private hospital — where producers, sponsors, and network executives couldn't find him. Then he would invite all of his cronies up for a non-stop party. Once, after several days of such goings-on, Gleason went to the nurses' station and announced, "I'm checking out and going home." When the head nurse asked him why, Gleason shrugged, "I'm not feeling so well."

FACING PAGE: **JACKIE GLEASON, AUDREY MEADOWS,**
                           ART CARNEY, JOYCE RANDOLPH

THIS PAGE: **ELAINE STRITCH, PERT KELTON**

FOLLOWING PAGE: **BILL CULLEN, JAYNE MEADOWS, STEVE ALLEN**

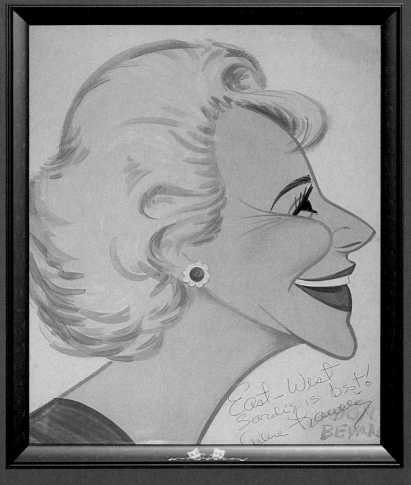

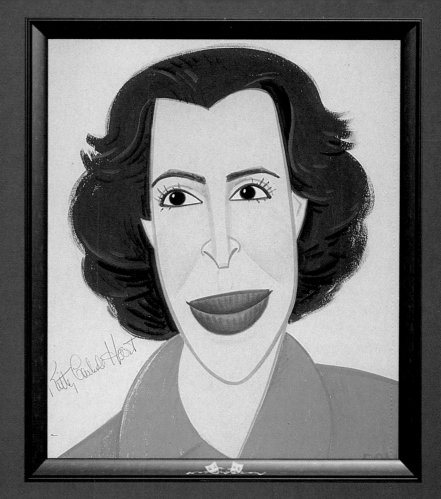

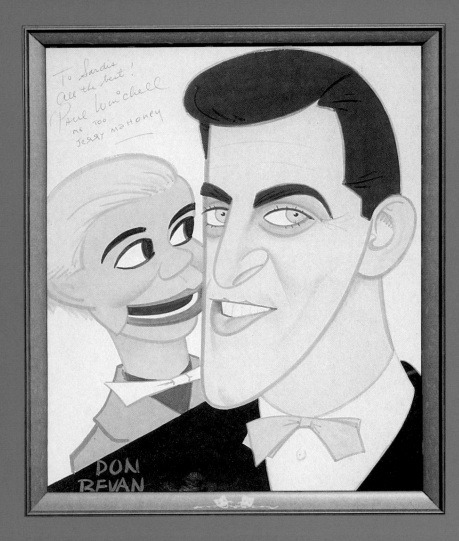

Soon after I took over the restaurant from Dad, I started another one of Sardi's long-running traditions: a radio show, which originated live from the dining room on the second floor. *Luncheon At Sardi's* started on March 8, 1947, and broadcast almost uninterruptedly until just a couple of years ago, making it one of the longest-running radio shows of all time. For a while it was a television show as well, but it continued all those years on WOR Radio.

The first host was Bill Slater, and then Bill was succeeded by his ad-man brother Tom, who was succeeded by Ray Heatherton. The show then went off the air for a short time, to be revived with Arlene Francis as the hostess. The charming and witty Arlene continued by herself, while appearing in a number of shows on and off Broadway and as a regular panelist on *What's My Line*. During the last years of the program Arlene was joined by Joan Hamburg.

Over the decades we had all kinds of guests on the show, from athletes to opera stars, politicians to crooners. We always had a live audience eating their lunch during the broadcasts. When guests went on the air, they had to cross the dining room to the platform where the interviewers sat. Before too long that short stroll became the radio equivalent of an opening night entrance into the downstairs dining room — stars could tell how popular they were by the gasps and whispers they generated when they appeared.

Before he teamed up with Imogene Coca on TV, Sid Caesar made one of his first radio appearances on our show. In fact, Imogene Coca often appeared on *Luncheon At Sardi's* when she was a solo cabaret entertainer. One day, she came in looking quite forlorn. She explained to Bill Slater that she had just paid quite a bit of money for some song arrangements, and had left them in a taxi on her way to the broadcast. The next day, one of our listeners brought the arrangements to the restaurant.

Basil Rathbone appeared on the show one day, and before he went on the air, a fan came up to him and cried, "Oh, my God, it's Rasil Bathbone!" Rathbone was unperturbed. "I've been called everything," he assured the woman, "including Basal Metabolism."

PREVIOUS PAGE: **ARLENE FRANCIS, KITTY CARLISLE HART, BENNETT CERF, PEGGY CASS**

THIS PAGE: **PAUL WINCHELL & JERRY MAHONEY, MITCH MILLER**

100

Paul Winchell, the popular ventriloquist, generally let his dummy Jerry Mahoney do all the talking; Tony Curtis revealed that he had once been a shoeshine boy, and his favorite location was just outside of Sardi's front door.

Another long-running theatrical tradition started at Sardi's: the Antoinette Perry ("Tony") Awards. Antoinette Perry started out in the theater as a child actress, and became a leading lady in the 'teens and 'twenties. One of the plays she starred in was *The Ladder* in 1926 — a play about reincarnation that ran over a year, only because a Texas oil man sank half a million dollars into it. Near the end of the run, people were actually being paid to see it.

Miss Perry later gained genuine fame as one of Broadway's first female directors, helming such productions as *Harvey* and Preston Sturges' *Strictly Dishonorable*. "Tony" was instrumental in organizing the American Theater Wing, which operated the Stage Door Canteen during the war.

When she died in 1946, her many friends and admirers wanted to memorialize her in some significant way. John Golden, who practically lived in Sardi's, was having lunch (probably ordering his favorite, *moules marinière*) with Jacob Wilk, the film-company executive, when the idea of the "Tony" was born. Mr. Golden conveyed the suggestion to friends on the board of the American Theater Wing, who set about creating an award for excellence in the theater in Tony's memory.

Among the first "Tony" winners in 1947 were many Sardi's regulars, including José Ferrer, Helen Hayes, Ingrid Bergman, Patricia Neal and Elia Kazan — who still refuses to let us do his caricature. The award committee also honored Dad. My parents had just taken their first vacation since Dad retired, and were in California when a telegram arrived announcing that Dad was being cited — and, needless to say, Mother and Dad were on the next flight back to New York.

At that time, the statuettes that are handed out today hadn't been designed, so Dad received a gold money clip with the inscription, "To Vincent Sardi, for providing a transient home and comfort for theater folks at Sardi's for twenty years." (I was similarly honored at a Tony Dinner in 1983.)

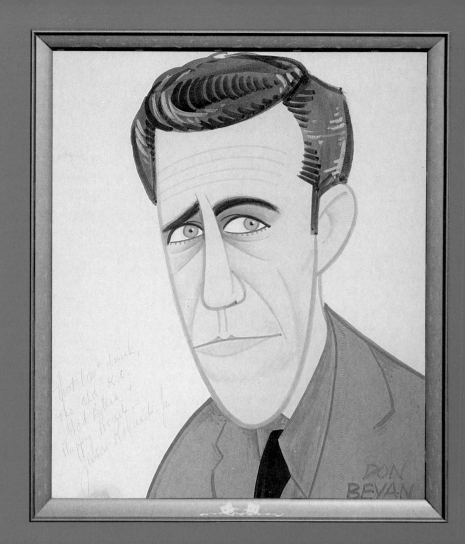

THIS PAGE: JASON ROBARDS, CHRISTOPHER PLUMMER

FOLLOWING PAGE: WALTER MATTHAU, JACK LEMMON

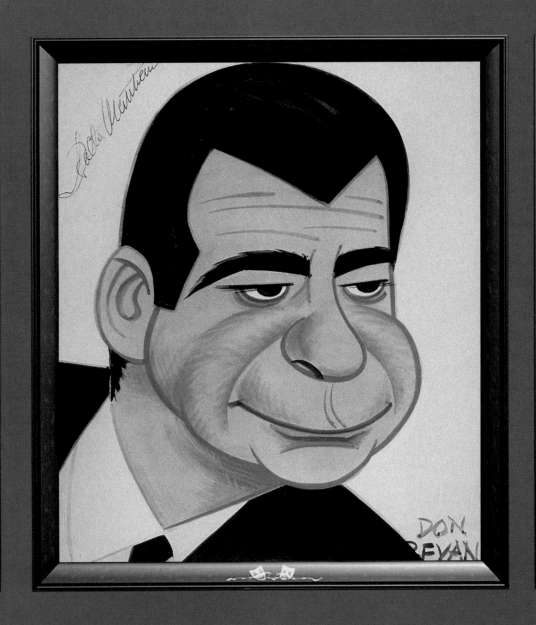

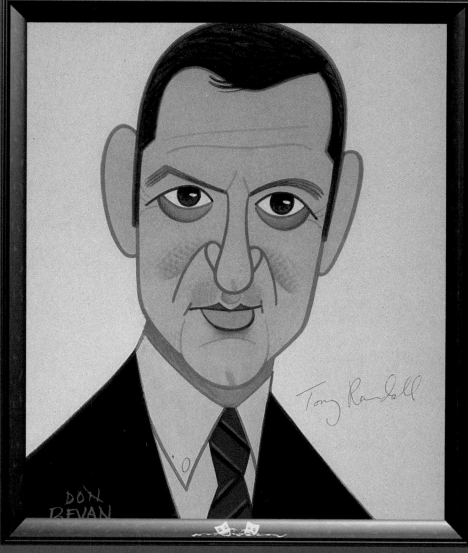

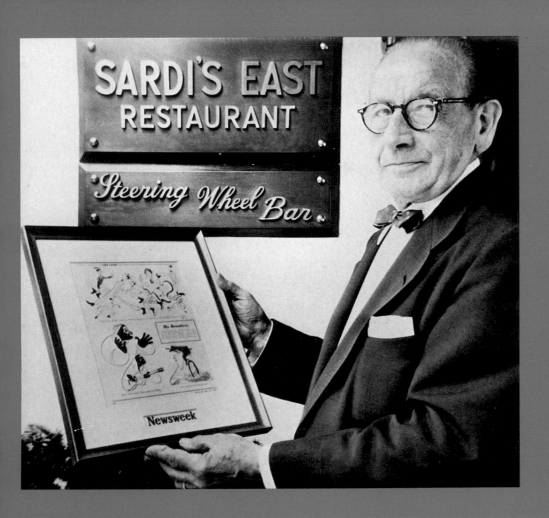

gallon and was known to hit a top speed of forty miles per hour with a good tail wind.

There was a barge owner who was willing to float the bus all the way north to Paulsboro, New Jersey, provided we got it to him in Jacksonville. Once in New Jersey, the bus seemed farther away than ever. We consulted cartographers and the New Jersey Highway authorities about how to get it into Manhattan. The good folks from New Jersey banned it from all major highways — just because it would only do forty miles per hour and couldn't clear the overpasses. So I rounded up a group of friends and headed for Paulsboro with a fifteen-foot pole. (All right, I suppose I can't let this one pass by — nobody would touch the thing with a ten-foot pole.)

We snaked around the back country roads, stopped at every overpass, measured the clearance with the pole, and felt

I opened a second restaurant called Sardi's East in 1958. Dad had retired, of course, but I persuaded him to man the door there, and I think he enjoyed it immensely. We had three rooms: the Steering Wheel Bar, which was decorated in a sports car motif (one of my great passions outside the restaurant is racing cars), the Vintage Room and the Theater Room. I asked Al Hirschfeld to decorate the Theater Room. Al Created a black and white wallpaper out of his own caricatures. Well, we had the paper printed, and when we put it on the walls, it was clear that Al's work was never meant to be appreciated on such a scale. After all the expense and trouble, we painted over Hirschfeld's work

The biggest problem for us on the east side was getting diners to the theater in time for the curtain across town. In 1961 I got wind of the perfect solution: a double-decker London bus. This magnificent carriage had been shipped to Florida in 1952 as part of a promotion by the British Travel Authority. The price was right — $3,000 — and I knew there was nothing else quite like it in New York at the time. I just had to buy it. All I had to do was get the bus here from Miami. It got three miles to the

our way along. On the front of the bus, we'd pasted a sign that said "Sardi's or Bust." By the time we crept over the George Washington Bridge and coasted to a halt in front of the restaurant for a photo opportunity, the poor bus was ready for about $2,000 in repairs, and must have been homesick for Piccadilly Circus.

The double decker was a huge hit. It made its first run on the opening night of Noel Coward's *Sail Away*. Among its first passengers from the East Side to the Theater District were Coward himself, Elaine Stritch, the star of the show, Elsa Maxwell, Leonard Lyons and the Lunts.

Tyrone Guthrie actually petitioned me to open a Sardi's in Minneapolis. Guthrie was feeling some incipient homesickness before leaving to start his theater out there. And while

THIS PAGE: THE DOUBLE DECKER BUS AT HOTEL ASTOR,
                      THE BUS AT SARDI'S EAST

FOLLOWING PAGE: WERNER KLEMPERER, EDDIE ALBERT, DANNY
                      AIELLO, MILDRED NATWICK, FRED GWYNNE

Guthrie kept asking, I kept smiling and saying, "No!" If we had trouble drawing crowds in the wilds of the East Side, I figured, what shot would we have at a long run in Minnesota?

George Grizzard had been lured out of Edward Albee's *Who's Afraid of Virginia Woolf* to play the title role in Guthrie's production of *Hamlet* in Minneapolis (which also starred Hume Cronyn and Jessica Tandy). Grizzard wanted to pick the brain of the most celebrated Hamlet of the century, so he invited Sir John Gielgud to lunch at Sardi's. They were discussing the finer points of the role when Guthrie spotted them, strode to their table — all six-feet-six-inches of him — and asked, "Will the real Hamlet please stand up?"

Pint-sized producer Billy Rose hadn't actually backed *Virginia Woolf*, but because it played in the Billy Rose Theater on 41st Street (now called the Nederlander), Rose always referred to it as "my play." Billy Rose was appalled that Grizzard would leave the cast of a hit play to go to Minneapolis, and confronted the actor. "But, Billy," pleaded Grizzard. "it's *Hamlet*!" Billy Rose wasn't impressed: "Oh, you actors! *Hamlet* — it's like Hedy Lamarr blowing hot in your ear, right?"

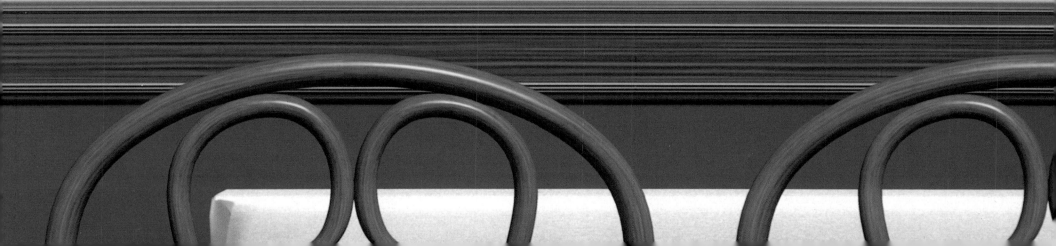

In 1974, Don Bevan announced that he was retiring from the post of Sardi's caricaturist. To find his successor, I held a public competition, and asked artists to submit their portfolios. I selected the cream of the crop, and assigned each one of the final candidates a different celebrity to caricature.

One of the contenders was Brooklyn native Richard Baratz, who had been working as a note and certificate engraver for the American Bank Note Company. His subject was Bette Midler, who was appearing on Broadway at the time in her *Clams on the Half Shell Revue*. When the finished caricatures came back, it was clear that Midler's was the best — not only was it a brilliant caricature, but "The Divine Miss M" had refused to sign it. Not that I was after another Gard, but it takes a really good caricaturist to offend his subject. After all, for an actor, having your caricature done is like a bad review from a critic; asking an actor what he thinks about critics is like asking a fire hydrant what it thinks about dogs.

I had Richard Baratz tackle another Richard: Burton. Don Bevan had done Burton before, of course, but, like so many others (including a fine one of Barbra Streisand), it had been stolen. Burton was in town to take over the leading role in *Equus* from his fellow Welshman Anthony Hopkins. Burton had been signed to do the movie of the play and wanted the experience of playing the role on stage.

Baratz was a bit star-struck at the beginning of his tenure, but he wasn't really prepared for the reception he got. He had arranged to meet Burton backstage before a show, about 6:30 in the evening. When he went to the theater, there was already a crowd standing six deep around the stage door. Mr. Baratz isn't a very tall fellow, and he was having trouble making his way to the door, when a guard with a bullhorn came out and bellowed, "Is there a Richard Baratz in the crowd?"

The multitudes parted like the Red Sea, and Baratz strolled into the theater, shaking like a leaf. A number of famous people, including David Frost and Robert Goulet, were waiting for Burton, and Baratz was escorted right past them into Burton's dressing room. As you might expect, Burton was very gracious, had a long talk with Baratz, offered him a drink, let Baratz take as many photographs as he wanted, and joked, "Do anything you want with my face, but please don't draw my pockmarks!"

PREVIOUS PAGE:	JEAN STAPLETON, CARROLL O'CONNOR, BEATRICE ARTHUR, PAUL SORVINO, JACK WESTON, VINCENT GARDENIA
THIS PAGE:	RICHARD BARATZ BY BARATZ, AL PACINO
FACING PAGE:	RICHARD BURTON, GEORGE C. SCOTT, DUSTIN HOFFMAN, ROBERT DENIRO

Richard Burton.

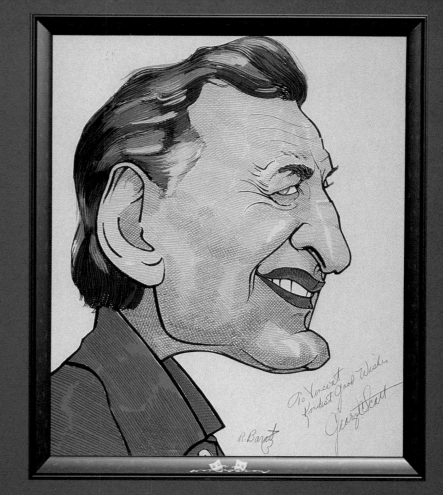

To Vincent Kindest Good Wishes George Scott

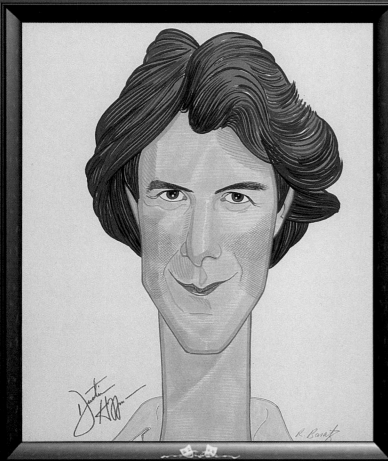

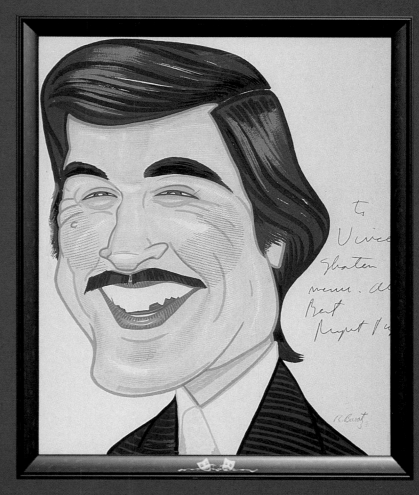

To Vincent Shaten menu. All Best Roger [?]

Richard puts it best: "True caricature is, let's face it, rather insulting, biting even; and you have to have a sense of humor about it. A lot of people are very vain. You're always dealing with egos, and some of them won't sign anything that isn't flattering. If the people are warm and have a sense of humor about them, it's more fun and easier to draw them. I have more success with the drawing. The first version is always the best, because it's my genuine instincts. The second or third version is harder. I'm holding back.

"The success of a drawing has a lot to do with the personality of the individual. In caricature, it's not just the face. It can be a certain look. There may be a certain look in the eye, or a certain way the person laughs. I go after that suggestion and exaggerate it."

Richard started doing caricatures as a student at the School of Visual Arts — not that they offer any courses in the art of caricature. But after several months of life classes, he found his fellow art students drawing the nude models more interesting and alive than the models themselves. And so a caricaturist was born.

Although Richard does serious paintings and graphic works, he has also had political cartoons and caricatures published in *The New York Times*, *The Daily News*, and *Rolling Stone*.

If you look carefully at Richard's work, you'll see his background as a bank note engraver coming out. The detail in his work is fantastic. He does a lot of intricate cross-hatching, which gives the caricatures a very rich look, even from a distance. It also makes his work totally different from both Bevan's and Gard's. Each of them had developed a very distinct personal style, and Richard's was just as distinctive. The only drawback about Richard Baratz back then was the fact that he really didn't know people in the theater.

THIS PAGE: BERNARD JACOBS, GERALD SCHOENFELD, A.M. ROSENTHAL

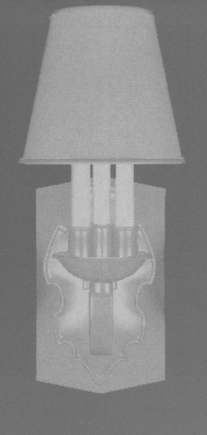

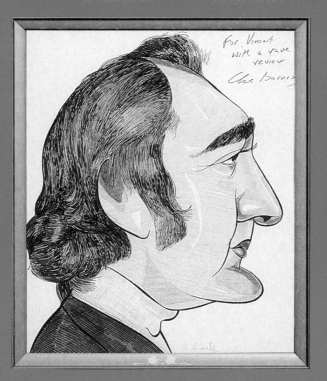

One of the first people I sent Richard to caricature was Bernard Jacobs, who with his partner Gerald Schoenfeld, runs the Shubert Organization. Well, Richard, being new to the business, didn't know who Bernie Jacobs was. Somehow he confused him with a chap named *Ben* Jacobs. Now, Ben Jacobs was a very old man who had been a fight promoter, and he still had a dingy office over on Eleventh Avenue.

Richard went over there and did a very good caricature, got it signed, and brought it back to me, holding it out for inspection. I looked at it, read the inscription, which was a very heartfelt tribute to Dad, and said, "Richard, it's very good, but who the hell is Ben Jacobs?" Richard realized his mistake, but said, "Mr. Sardi, I don't know how to tell you this, but Ben Jacobs and his whole family are on their way over to Sardi's right now to toast the caricature!" What else could I do but put dear old Ben Jacobs up on the wall?

Soon after, Richard did the right fellow. *This*, for the record, is Bernard Jacobs. (And Gerald Schoenfeld, too — along with one of our neighbors, A.M. Rosenthal of *The New York Times*.)

Richard makes an appointment to meet the star in person; he takes as many photographs as he can; then he goes home and works from the photos. He also likes to have his own photograph taken with each subject; he gets an autograph as well, so Richard has an enviable personal collection.

When he started at Sardi's, Richard noticed the autograph collectors who spend hours and hours outside stage doors and in front of the restaurant waiting for just one brief shining moment with their idols. Not long ago, the great Russian ballerina Tamara Geva was leaving Sardi's when a flock of autograph hunters swooped upon her, asking, "Are you somebody famous? Are you a star?" Miss Geva deftly quipped, "I'm a retired circus acrobat." They left her alone.

THIS PAGE: **CLIVE BARNES, LIZ SMITH**

FOLLOWING PAGE: **LILY TOMLIN, JOAN RIVERS, WHOOPI GOLDBERG**

Along with autographs and photographs, Richard also enjoys collecting stories. He was photographing Rex Reed, who lives in the Dakota apartments on West 72nd Street (the location for *Rosemary's Baby*). One of Rex's neighbors was Mrs. Boris Karloff. Karloff, from a distinguished British consular family, was the first actor to be allowed to move into the Dakota (albeit to a basement room at first). Soon after Karloff's death, Rex Reed expressed his condolences to Mrs. Karloff, saying how sorry he was that he'd never actually met the horror-film star. "Don't worry," Mrs. Karloff assured Rex, "he'll be back."

Victor Borge was another early caricature by Baratz. This anything-but-melancholy Dane has a smile that can light up a room. Borge was entering the restaurant on a beautiful April day, and one of our waiters said, "Spring in the air, Mr. Borge," and Victor said, "Oh, all right, if you insist," and sprang about three feet into the air. When Richard Baratz met Victor Borge backstage at Carnegie Hall to photograph him, Borge took him by the arm and said, "Step into my dressing room, Mr. Baratz," and led Richard into the men's room.

Richard Harris held the curtain during the Broadway revival of *Camelot* so that Richard Baratz could photograph him. Baratz had been waiting in the wings for Harris to arrive, but Harris

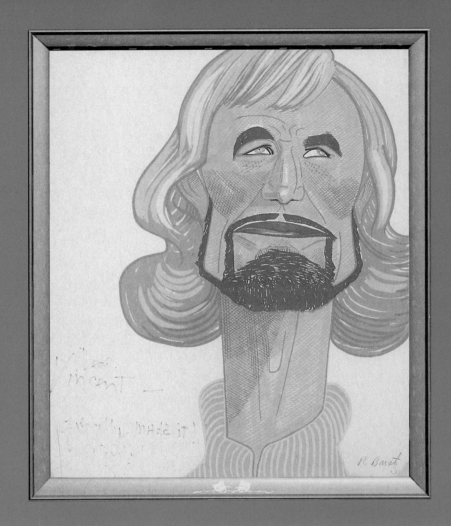

came into the theater right before curtain time. Baratz offered to wait until after the show, but Harris said, "Let them wait — the only reason I did this bloody show on Broadway is so I could get my picture hung at Sardi's!"

There was one fellow, a very prominent Hollywood leading man (who shall remain nameless and whose picture isn't in this book) who was starring on Broadway, who just wouldn't sign Richard Baratz's caricature of him. Richard kept going back, toning down the amount of caricature until he was presenting the star with the fourth or fifth version, which was not a caricature but a rather flattering portrait. The star still wouldn't sign. He finally took Richard's drawing pad and started to sketch himself, saying, "Richard, it's simple. Do it just like this."

Richard was spoiled early on by Liza Minnelli. When he went to her apartment, she opened the door and gave Richard a big hug and a kiss, as if she'd known him all her life. She put

PREVIOUS PAGE: MYRNA LOY, LIZA MINNELLI, BEVERLY SILLS, SHIRLEY MACLAINE

THIS PAGE: MARVIN HAMLISCH, RICHARD HARRIS

114

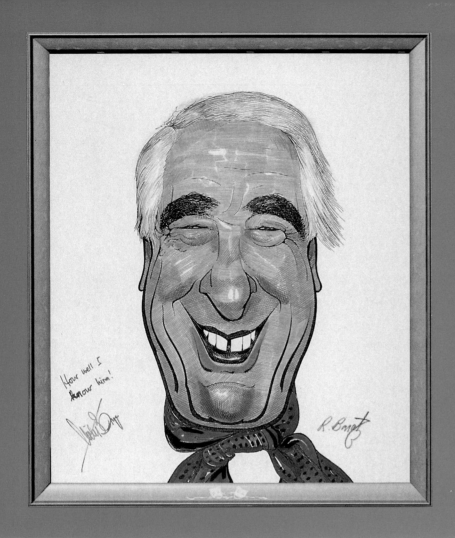

roe and John Garfield, as well as a prized set of caricatures by Enrico Caruso (who was a caricaturist before he was a singer), all the while feeding Richard apple strudel.

Dom DeLuise met Richard in Dom's old neighborhood at *his* mother's house. Dom brought his family into the restaurant to toast the caricature when it was hung on the wall. He still sends Richard Christmas cards. Richard didn't know quite to expect when he met Margaret Hamilton — T*he Wizard of Oz*'s Wicked Witch — but he found her to be one of the gentlest, sweetest people he had ever met, as everyone did. Al Pacino was very nervous about meeting Richard — very quiet, and very shy. He didn't much like publicity, but was happy with Richard's work.

Now that Richard has been our caricaturist for so many years, and has added so many new faces to the walls, we've "retired" a lot of Gard's older ones — many of them in delicate or fragile condition — to the Library of the Performing Arts at Lincoln Center, which is an amazing treasure trove of irreplaceable theater history and artifacts.

Richard right at ease, and he felt completely at home with Liza. She loved her caricature, signed it happily, and I don't think Richard has seen her since. But the warmth shows in her caricature, I think. Richard quickly found out what Mother and Dad knew from the very beginning: actors are human. Years ago, however, someone made that same comment to George S. Kaufman, who retorted, "Oh, yeah? Did you ever eat with one?"

Richard met Marvin Hamlisch at his mother's house. While Richard was snapping pictures of the Oscar- and Tony-winning composer, Marvin's mother kept asking him to take out the garbage. Richard was also charmed by the fact that Jane Seymour has different-colored eyes: one is brown and one is green. He says that she has one of the most gorgeous eyes he's ever seen, but he won't tell me which one.

Lee Strasberg showed Richard his collection of autographs, memorabilia and oil paintings by friends such as Marilyn Mon-

THIS PAGE: VICTOR BORGE, DOM DELUISE

FOLLOWING PAGE: MIA FARROW, MICHAEL CRAWFORD (AS THE PHANTOM OF THE OPERA), JONATHAN PRYCE, JANE SEYMOUR, GREGORY HINES, BILLY JOEL

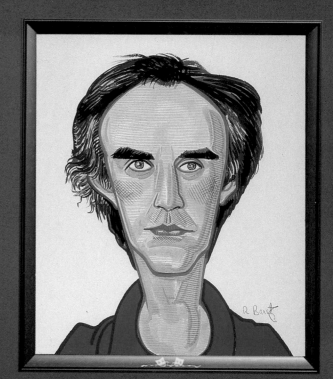

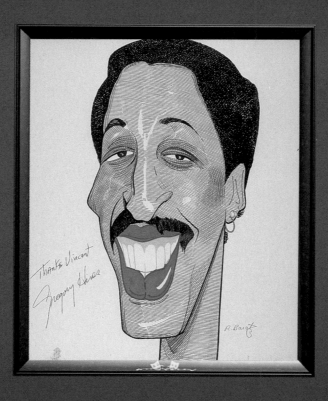

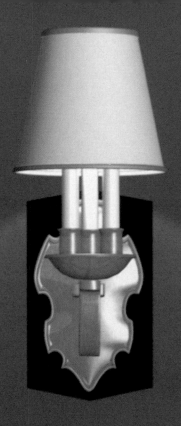

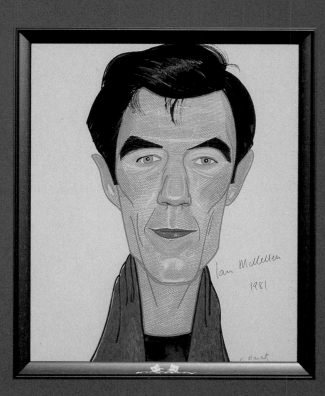

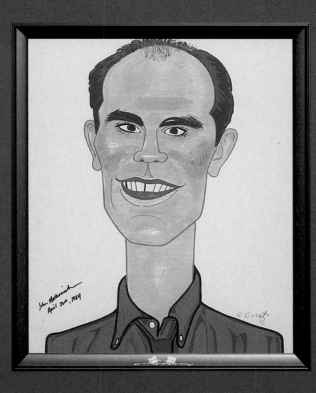

People always ask me, "Who was the most impressive person you ever met in Sardi's?" I have to admit that, although I love all of the people of the theater who have made Sardi's a second home, some of the most impressive people weren't in show business at all: President Harry Truman, Eleanor Roosevelt, General Omar Bradley — but one of my favorite people of all time has to be Ernie Kovacs.

I didn't meet Ernie in connection with the restaurant or any aspect of the entertainment world. He and I became pals because of our mutual love of racing cars. At the time, I was driving a Jaguar XK120, and Ernie had just bought an Allard — both English cars imported for the first time after World War II. Ernie told me once that he loved nothing better than driving his Allard through the back roads of Connecticut, seated on the "wrong" side of the road (since the Allard was English), low to the ground, reaching out and picking wildflowers as he went. If you can imagine Ernie Kovacs — with that black hair, that black mustache, and that face that looked like a buccaneer's with a cigar stuck in his mouth — picking wildflowers in a sports car, you can't help but see the incongruity of his character.

When Ernie had an early morning live TV show, he often got stuck for guests, and he'd call me in to come over and cook

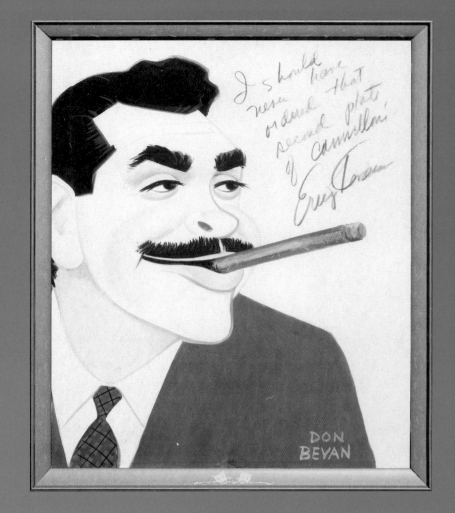

something on the air. One morning when Ernie called I decided to make some Veal Scallopine and a new California-born salad that had just hit New York: the Caesar Salad. At 6:30 a.m., I showed up at the studio with the salad makings, the veal and a bottle of sherry. Ernie watched me start the Caesar Salad, but when I broke the egg, mixed it with Parmesan cheese and anchovies, Ernie took one look at the mess in the salad bowl and gulped, "God, Vincent, it's too early for this. What else do you have?" I showed him the veal and the sherry, and he said, "Good. Open that sherry and let's drink it!"

Around that time, Ernie was fighting a bitter, drawn-out battle to regain custody of his children, who had been taken by Ernie's ex-wife to Florida, where Ernie couldn't find them. He literally spent every cent he made on private detectives trying to trace his kids and get them back. All the while, he was creating some of the most innovative comedy television has ever

PREVIOUS PAGE: TYNE DALY, SIR IAN MCKELLEN, GLENN CLOSE, JOHN MALKOVICH, SWOOSIE KURTZ

THIS PAGE: VINCENT SARDI, JR. WITH BROOKS ATKINSON, ERNIE KOVACS

table where we sat, and it was a delight to speak with such a handsome family, so appreciative of my teacher, Mrs. [Anne Sullivan] Macy, and all she had done to restore my human heritage … It saddens me to think that I have not had leisure to 'fleet the golden time carelessly' at Mr. Sardi's in many a year."

We've survived a lot over the last seventy years at Sardi's, everything from talkies and the first Stock Market Crash and the "Great Depression" through fires (a fire closed the kitchen in 1970, after which I ran out and found Mama Zoi, a babushka-wearing neighborhood hot dog vendor and set her up in the lobby until we could get the kitchen going again) to a recent sale of the restaurant that went sour (and the resulting court battle to re-open), but Sardi's is still here, and I hope it will stay here as long as there are opening nights to toast and flops to mourn and theater people in the Theater District who can still say, "Meet me — where else? — at Sardi's."

seen. I had nothing but admiration for Ernie. Behind his wild clowning and outwardly reckless manner, Ernie was a tense and worried man, suffering from severe intestinal bleeding. I let him run up quite a tab in the restaurant, and one day Ernie came to me and must have thought he was paying me the ultimate compliment: "Vincent, I owe you a lot of money. Since we're such good friends, I just wanted you to know that you'll be the last person I repay."

I must say, after he had straightened out his personal affairs and married the lovely Edie Adams, he did pay the bill — then bought Edie a white Rolls-Royce.

Another fond memory is of Helen Keller, who used to come in often when I was a boy. Years later she wrote to Dad: "Whenever we entered Mr. Sardi's cozy restaurant, we felt the warmth of his interest not only as a host, but also as a friend … he would bring Mrs. Sardi and their two beautiful children to the

THIS PAGE: HELEN KELLER, VINCENT SARDI, JR. WITH
                      ELIZABETH TAYLOR

FOLLOWING PAGE: VINCENT SARDI, JR. BY BARATZ